Praise for *Authentic Sales Leadership*

"This isn't a book. It's the bible! The bible for sales team leadership and performance."

–John Rossman, Author of *Big Bet Leadership*,
The Amazon Way, and *Think Like Amazon*

"JT Turner's *Authentic Sales Leadership* is a practical and insightful guide for sales leaders at all levels. With a focus on authenticity, culture, and execution, Turner shares his hard-won wisdom from decades of experience building and leading successful sales teams. This book is a valuable resource for anyone looking to create a high-performing sales organization."

–Richard A. Moran, Ph.D., bestselling author of
Never Say Whatever and former CEO

"There are thousands of leadership books you can buy. But this one is different and better and more applicable. *Authentic Sales Leadership* is a must-read for sales executives and business leaders who are serious about building and leading high-performing teams. His insights on building a championship team-oriented culture, leading from the front, and navigating the complexities of modern sales organizations make this book an invaluable resource for anyone looking to elevate their leadership impact. Highly recommended for current leaders or those hoping to break into leadership."

–Jim Dougherty, Senior Lecturer at MIT Sloan, 5x CEO,
start-up founder and Business Executive

Authentic Sales Leadership is a must-read playbook for anyone looking to lead with authenticity while driving performance and scaling teams. John 'JT' Turner shares real-world insights every CRO and sales leader can use to build a culture of excellence and accountability.

–Mark Wayland, Chief Revenue Officer, Box

"John 'JT' Turner is an authentic leader who knows how to drive growth while leading a culture of accountability, resilience, and winning. Having had the pleasure of working with JT firsthand, I have seen his leadership principles in action—his ability to inspire teams, execute, and create a championship mentality is second to none. If you are serious about building and leading a world-class organization, the practical lessons recounted in this book make it an essential read."

–Burton Goldfield, Retired president and CEO (NYSE: TNET), corporate board member

"*Authentic Sales Leadership* is a must-read for anyone looking to build and lead high-performing sales teams. John 'JT' Turner's practical, no-nonsense approach—rooted in discipline, accountability, and culture—aligns with what truly drives lasting success."

–Jay Tyler, Founder and principal, Jay Tyler Consulting

Sales leadership is about inspiring people, building culture, and driving results with purpose. In *Authentic Sales Leadership*, John 'JT' Turner delivers a clear, experience-driven playbook that aligns perfectly with the principles of value-based selling.

–Julie Thomas, CEO, ValueSelling Associates, and bestselling author of *ValueSelling*

Authentic leadership is the foundation of every great sales organization, and John 'JT' Turner has written the ultimate guide to mastering it. *Authentic Sales Leadership* is packed with real-world insights and timeless lessons every sales leader needs to build high-performance teams and drive sustainable success.

–Gerhard Gschwandtner, Founder and CEO, *Selling Power Magazine*

"In *Authentic Sales Leadership*, John "JT" Turner distills decades of frontline experience into practical, principled guidance for developing effective sales leaders. A valuable resource for students and professionals alike."

–Professor Chuck Byers, Leavey School of Business, Santa Clara University

"*Authentic Sales Leadership* nails what most books miss—real, in-the-trenches leadership that drives repeatable, scalable growth. JT has built and led teams that win. This is the playbook every founder and sales leader should have on their desk."

— Tim Connors, Founder, PivotNorth Capital

AUTHENTIC SALES LEADERSHIP

PROVEN TACTICS TO BUILD AND LEAD CHAMPIONSHIP TEAMS

John "JT" Turner

ISBN: 979-8-89079-257-0 (hardcover)
ISBN: 979-8-89079-258-7 (paperback)
ISBN: 979-8-89079-259-4 (ebook)

Design by Jetlaunch Publishing

This book is dedicated to:

Mom and Dad, you made me who I am.

Amy, WE did this.

A.M.D.G.

"Pay attention.
Be astonished.
Tell about it."
—Mary Oliver

Table of Contents

Foreword

John 'JT' Turner is an incredible sales leader! I feel honored to have worked with him and seen him become a seasoned C-suite executive and have had the pleasure of knowing and working with John for over twenty years. His energy, passion, and enthusiasm are infectious, really motivating the people around him. His boundless energy and positivity means he inspires those others to achieve results, his peers, stakeholders, and the teams he leads.

In addition to delivering outstanding results himself, John has also helped create many leaders who have gone on in their careers to become C-suite executives themselves. It is the ultimate confirmation of true leadership that John has developed others to be so successful.

It is a privilege to read this book as John has openly shared his own real-life lessons of his career journey, giving genuine examples of positive success in a tough sales business environment. He describes all of this while demonstrating how he pays attention to the important things, such as focusing on people and culture. He shares his personal true story being authentic and describes his own learning along the way, and he talks about how he does this differently while driving sustainable results and lasting change.

The book is easy to read and packed full of stories to make it come alive.

Enjoy the read—I did!

Mandy Flint
International Leadership/Cultural Change Strategist, CEO/ board C-suite advisor/coach. Preparing CEOs for the role. Amazon bestselling author of four books and fourteen awards, published by FT/Pearson

My Story

After I graduated from Santa Clara University, I thought I wanted to be a banker like my father had been. So, I explored different opportunities at the job fair during my senior year. One that particularly interested me was the First Interstate Bank training program. It was the one I was most excited about. When I went to the desk to sign up for an interview, the person there said, "I'm sorry; this is only for people with a GPA of 3.5 or above." I smiled and asked, "Are you sure about that? Would you mind double-checking, just in case?" She looked at it more closely and realized that the 3.5 requirement was for a different position. She had been turning people down all day, but I was able to secure the interview. I felt like maybe things were going my way.

After a series of interviews, I had a final interview with the hiring manager in Northern California, San Francisco. The meeting was scheduled for late in the day, so I had plenty of time to get a haircut in the morning to prepare. It was the only company I had applied to. I was confident I would nail the interview.

I went to the barbershop in my hometown, the one I'd been going to since my father took me as a kid. While I was getting my haircut, two of the barbers got into an argument and started pushing and shoving each other. It was crazy! I finally had to step in between them to stop the fight and ensure my haircut could be finished so I could make it to the interview on time. As it was, I had to run to the train, sprint to the office and climb eight flights of stairs. When I arrived at the interview, I was a sweaty mess from the run, so I slipped into the men's bathroom to try to towel off.

The interviewer was very personable and didn't mention anything about my state and instead asked me about being a four year walk on to the Santa Clara University Division 1 basketball team. We had just defeated Pepperdine University to win the league title, and I was bragging about it. She then mentioned she was a Pepperdine graduate. I worried that I had just blown the interview in the first five minutes. However, she had a good attitude, and a few weeks later, I found out I got the job.

I began in the management training program at First Interstate Bank. I admired how my father had an impact on the community. At his funeral five years earlier the church was so full that people lined the streets. These were the people in the community that he had helped. It inspired me to do the same. This desire to help people has affected my leadership style throughout my career.

I spent seven years in the banking industry, ultimately becoming a vice president at Chase Manhattan Bank, working in their private banking group with mortgages for high-net-worth individuals. During this time, I worked with many successful people in Silicon Valley and learned firsthand how they made money. The desire for similar financial success drove my transition to the technology industry.

I interviewed with all the big tech companies in Silicon Valley at that time—Oracle, HP, Sun, Silicon Graphics—and they all told me, "You're a banker; you don't know anything about technology. Stay in banking." But I was determined, so I joined a small reseller and took a 100 percent commission job. This was one of the best things I could have done at this point in my career. During this period, I also invested in myself by earning my MBA at night and participating in my local Toastmasters group. It was a great experience. I learned a lot and gained confidence in myself as a businessman and a speaker.

After my first year at the reseller, a leader at Digital Equipment Corporation, a major technology company at the time, took a risk on me and hired me as a sales rep. I will always be grateful to her. I spent a year there learning the industry while also taking the Dale Carnegie Sales Excellence course. Two attendees from the course recommended me for a sales job at the technology research company Gartner. During the interview process, I met some of their sales leaders, and they were different from any leaders I had met before. They recognized something in me that I knew I had but never fully realized in the banking industry. Gartner had a competitive environment and invested heavily in their salespeople and they expected that I would excel in their program.

The process to get the job was rigorous, but ultimately, they selected me and assigned me the lowest-producing territory on the team, as that's where new hires typically started. I fully immersed myself in the role, working hard to master the sales pitch and methodology. I drove significant activity in my territory, often bringing sales managers on calls with me to learn from their expertise. This is where my career really took off. Gartner had a strong sales culture and was a fantastic company. They invested in their people and had great leaders who recognized potential and taught the craft of selling.

In my first year of selling, I earned the Eagle Award, which was given to the top 1 percent of all salespeople in the global organization. During that time, they also put me through a training program they had created called the Management Awareness Program (MAP). It was an incredible experience and introduced me to management.

Top sales manager at Gartner

After my first year, my manager decided to leave the company to pursue a bigger opportunity, and I was immediately promoted to district manager. I led a team of eight people, some of whom had been my teammates, and I also hired new members. I'm not sure I always knew what I was doing, and maybe I was just lucky, but in my first year, we became the number one sales team at Gartner. This was during the dot-com boom in Silicon Valley.

In the meantime, I'm sure I made plenty of mistakes as a manager, but I brought passion and enthusiasm to the role. I spent three years as manager, then a new chief revenue officer joined the organization. One of the first things he did was create a chief of staff role, selecting one high-potential manager to spend a year with him, training, developing, and learning how to be a chief revenue officer. I'm not sure I ever wanted a job more than I wanted this one. I did everything I could to get the position and was ultimately selected. It was a pivotal moment because he was an excellent teacher with the highest values and morals. He was also incredibly intelligent—a person truly worth learning from. After the year was complete, I was assigned to a new business unit that was building a new sales team, the fastest-growing group at Gartner, which was another great experience.

The job was an incredible opportunity to build an organization from scratch. The problem was I traveled almost 100,000 miles in six months. Around that time, I received a call from my former manager, who was at the technology company VERITAS. The storage and

My last day at Gartner, happy to be off the road!

storage management company had acquired several businesses, and we saw an opportunity to grow those faster than the core product portfolio. When I started, I had ten people reporting to me. We grew the business tenfold through organic growth and further acquisitions.

Soon after I joined, we became part of what was, at that time, the largest software technology merger in history—between Symantec and VERITAS. I spent three years in this role, during which we grew the team and the business. Meanwhile, I applied for a promotion three times and was rejected each time. It was a humbling experience and ultimately led to my decision to leave Symantec. I publicly announced I would join a small startup as head of sales.

After I announced my departure, Symantec's chief revenue officer contacted me and said he had a job he wanted me to consider before I left. The role was to lead about a third of the European business, which would require me to move my family to Europe for two or three years to help build and lead the business. It was the opportunity of a lifetime and another inflection point in my career. So, I moved my young family to the UK, where I headed the technology sales organization for EMEA.

I wasn't necessarily well-received by the organization because it was highly technical, and I was not a technical person. Additionally, all the people who reported to me had either applied for or expressed interest in the job, so they had all wanted the role I now held. It was good timing that I read the book *Team of Rivals* about Abraham Lincoln, which tells the story of how, after being elected president, Lincoln asked several of his rivals to join his cabinet for the good of the Union.

I learned so much during that time. I visited thirty-one countries and got to know different cultures, different ways of doing business, and how business operates in Europe, the Middle East, and Africa. The goal of the role was to closely align the technical part of the organization with the sales organization. I learned how to listen, appreciate other people's viewpoints, and work with people from different cultures and backgrounds. It taught me a lot about building culture.

About six months into the job, I became overwhelmed. In my previous job, I had led about forty people. In this role, I had almost six hundred people reporting to me. I treated this organization like I was leading a small team. I couldn't focus, prioritize, or ensure I was spending time on the right things. I was likely close to failure when I was connected with an executive coach—the first I had ever worked with. She performed a 360° review and gave me feedback and coaching on what I was missing. It probably saved my job. I took the feedback and coaching seriously and changed the way I was leading, and it made a massive difference.

When I returned to the US, finding another role at Symantec was difficult. This is a typical issue when someone returns to headquarters from an international assignment. They are often forgotten, and finding a new role at that senior level often requires either leaving the company or having a new position created. I ended up having the great privilege and fun of working in the services organization, where I learned an incredible amount about how services and support organizations are run. It was an experience I have drawn upon many times since.

Soon after returning to the US and relocating my family, I used my experience and knowledge to build and lead my own sales organization. This led me to a company based in Long Island, NY. I believed they were creating disruptive technology in the backup and recovery market. The job also required a lot of travel, as I was building a new sales team to sell this new technology. However, the company wasn't delivering the technology, and I decided it was time to make a change. I had flown over 100,000 miles during my time there—all of it domestic—so I traveled a crazy amount while helping raise our two sons. It was exhausting work.

Ultimately, I was approached with an opportunity at TriNet, a small business HR cloud company based in San Leandro, California. It wasn't a company or industry I knew much about, but I decided to meet the CEO, Burton Goldfield, to learn more. From the minute we met at a coffee shop in Palo Alto, where we both had double espressos, I knew this was someone for which I wanted to work. The opportunity was to aggressively grow the sales organization and prove that it could grow organically, with the goal of eventually achieving an IPO.

It was my first big opportunity to join the CEO's table. Ultimately, we were able to quickly double the size of the sales organization, demonstrate organic growth, and integrate a few acquisitions, which led to us going public in 2014. It was the opportunity of a lifetime to help lead the company into the public markets.

I had a wonderful five-year run where we grew the business and built a great sales organization. We were selected as one of the best sales forces in American business by *Selling Power* magazine. I was especially proud of that accomplishment because I remembered my days as a sales rep at Gartner when they achieved similar awards, and I thought that maybe, someday, my team would achieve something like that.

When I decided it was time to leave TriNet, I was approached with an opportunity to help build a cybersecurity project at X, the moonshot factory. Little did I know how much that job and experience would change my career. Up to that point, I had a long sales career and learned many things. My time at X and Google would take that and turn it on its head, changing me for the better.

Then, I Ran into Google X and the Pandemic!

I left TriNet after a five-year run and ran into probably the most impactful time in my career: I was hired to work at Google X, the moonshot factory. It was an opportunity of a lifetime because it allowed me to be part of a team at X that built a cybersecurity project that ultimately became Chronicle and later became one of the foundational elements of the GCP security business unit. It was essentially taking thirty years of my business career and combining it into one of the world's most innovative groups within one of the most innovative companies. My time at Google allowed me to take all my business experience, apply it, and have it molded, transformed, and refined.

One of the many great things about working at X is that it's an incredibly collaborative place. They encourage and foster cross-collaboration, learning from each other, and learning different things. It allowed me to take all my business experience up to that point and completely open my mind to new ways of doing things. I can honestly say that my life has changed from my time at Google X and Google. It changed how I think and how I view things. Therefore, I will share what I learned in my business experience, what I learned at Google and Google X, and how that changed me moving forward.

I had the opportunity to work with people like Sergey Brin, Eric Schmidt, Vint Cerf, and Astro Teller. They all took a different interest in the projects at X and our project at Chronicle. During my short time with them, I learned so many things about how they looked at problems, asked questions, and gave feedback.

Google X is known as the moonshot factory because it's where Google builds and creates its most innovative projects. Projects like Waymo (the driverless car), drone delivery services, and other innovative projects were built out of X. The office is an old mall that has been converted into offices. It's a pretty exciting place. There are teams working on all kinds of innovative projects that are all given code names. Our project was named Lantern. It was a cybersecurity project that took Google's ability to process and search massive amounts of data and apply it to the cybersecurity problem.

I started with five people reporting to me and a mascot, a one-eyed French bulldog named Reggie. It was a fun and life-changing opportunity because Google X encourages so much innovation. My work there took everything I had learned up to that point and applied it in one of the world's most dynamic cultures. It was a unique opportunity for a sales leader to work inside X. The project became quite successful, and we spun out as an independent company, Chronicle, which was ultimately acquired by Google's GCP business unit and became the foundational element of the GCP security business unit. We grew from our first five to over one hundred people, yet we maintained our culture.

Many things I learned were modified, changed, and made better. I learned many lessons during that time.

I had a thirty-year career with many different experiences in different industries and parts of the world, and it culminated in this incredibly innovative place called Google and Google X that allowed me to take these lessons and apply them, and also learn different ways of doing things. It was almost like a career explosion between what I had done and this incredibly dynamic group. During the same time, the COVID pandemic hit us, which created even more opportunities for me to learn. Due to all these experiences, I decided to write this book to share the lessons I learned, how they changed me, and how you might apply them in your world.

Why Am I Writing This Book?

Thirty years ago, when my career was beginning, there were books (*How to Win Friends and Influence People, How to Become CEO, High Output Management, The Effective Executive, Wooden, and The Score Takes Care of Itself,* to name a few) that made a significant impact on me. They were practical, real-world advice from business leaders, written in a way I could easily understand and apply to my career. It's interesting to look back on those books now and see the notes I highlighted. (A mentor once told me never to read a book without a pen in my hand.) Many of these tips became fundamental to how I led and managed my career as a business leader. I would like to pass my knowledge on in an equally applicable way.

I will share what I've learned over time. I hope that some of this advice, recommendations, and lessons will be useful to a future generation of managers and business leaders, just as those books were for me many years ago.

What Has Changed Since My Career Started?

When I began my journey as a business leader, the environment was highly dictatorial and prescriptive. The traditional approach involved giving orders and expecting compliance, with the threat of termination for non-compliance. While the concept of the knowledge economy was discussed, the reality was more aligned with a command-and-control structure. However, over time, I've witnessed a significant shift in the dynamics of human potential and spirit. Individuals today desire autonomy, the ability to think for themselves, and a sense of control over their lives. They are no longer content being told what to do. Traditional leaders with an old-school mentality find it challenging to succeed in this evolving landscape. The days of dictating, yelling, and bullying are over; these approaches are no longer effective.

Before the pandemic, not only was there a growing desire among individuals to have greater control over their work, think for themselves, and experience more autonomy in their jobs, but they also sought purpose, mission, and impact in their work and a connection to something larger than themselves. Early in my career, there was less consideration given to how individual contributions fit into a broader picture.

However, the pandemic brought humanity to the forefront. We witnessed the vulnerability and resilience of people as they navigated personal losses, illness, and the challenges of working from home while juggling childcare and other responsibilities. The pandemic also highlighted the emotional toll on individuals and revealed that employees have lives outside of work.

I believe these changes have been a positive development. Instead of focusing solely on work-life balance, we now recognize the importance of viewing life as a whole. Our personal and professional lives should align, and we should bring our authentic selves to work. This approach has made management more challenging but also more rewarding. Leaders can foster growth and development by investing time in understanding individuals, their motivations, and their reasons for doing what they do. Simply telling someone what to do is no longer sufficient. Leaders must help their teams understand the purpose and significance of their work. This requires empathy, a deep understanding of people, and a consideration of what is in it for them.

Google X taught me it's ok to have fun

Leaders must also acknowledge their humanity. They need to be authentic and genuine, showing their true selves to their teams. This does not mean constantly displaying emotions, but it does involve admitting mistakes and acknowledging vulnerability. I hope this book's tone differs from what I would have written thirty years ago. Instead of being prescriptive and telling people what to do, I aim to share my learnings, tools, and mistakes so others can benefit from them. While some readers may not find all the content relevant, I hope they will find nuggets of wisdom that can be applied to their work.

It is important to acknowledge that when I began my career, the business world was predominantly white and male-dominated. Many of my early influencers and role models were white men, simply because that was the makeup of leadership at the time. Diverse role models were scarce, and I was not initially aware of the importance of diversity. However, as the world has become more diverse, so has my understanding of role models and the people I learn from. I have embraced the opportunity to learn from individuals from different backgrounds and perspectives. I am open to hearing about my mistakes and learning new things from my team. I am grateful for their patience and willingness to teach me.

I recognize that I am a work in progress and am always learning. I remain eager for new role models and people from whom I can learn. One such person is Dawn Staley, the coach of the University of South Carolina women's basketball team. She has built a successful program based on values, high standards, and teamwork. I have also learned a great deal from other role models, both public figures and colleagues from diverse backgrounds, particularly over the past five to ten years.

I look forward to continuing to learn from people from diverse backgrounds throughout the remainder of my career. I can confidently say that interacting, learning, and working with people from different backgrounds has enriched my career and life.

1

Sales Leadership Lessons I Learned From Google X and the Pandemic

Google X's Vision

X's mission is to invent and launch "moonshot" technologies to make the world a radically better place. X defines a moonshot as the intersection of a big problem, a radical solution, and breakthrough technology.

Don't Penalize Someone for Taking a Risk

At X, risk-taking is the name of the game. People come together with ideas to create moonshots. Creating a moonshot means you have a 99 percent chance of failure. One thing I loved about X was how they celebrated failures. They would base the celebration on Mexico's Día de los Muertos, or Day of the Dead, where they would have a ceremony to celebrate failed projects. The team who failed the project would be celebrated, and the lessons learned would be shared. Then, the team would be encouraged to move on to another project. What a great way to encourage creativity!

When I was at VERITAS, one of our sales engineers decided she wanted to go into sales and took a risk. She was a fantastic sales engineer but not a great salesperson. She was unsuccessful. I remember my manager at the time recommending we should fire her because she was unsuccessful in the role. I argued that nobody in the organization would ever take a risk like she did again if we fired her. Ultimately, we didn't fire her; we moved her back into a sales engineer role. Now, she has a senior position at another organization. I bet one of the reasons for her success is that she took a risk and was celebrated for taking it—not penalized.

Celebrate and encourage people in your organization who take risks. If they are talented but fail, don't penalize them; learn the lessons and give them another opportunity to take a risk. Nothing will kill an organization more than penalizing people who take risks.

Think 10X

I remember sitting at a round table with Astro Teller, the captain of Moonshots at X. As one of the few enterprise salespeople brought into X, I was fascinated by how he led an organization of a thousand of the world's brightest minds. While not an expert in sales, he was undoubtedly skilled at creating moonshots and organizations capable of realizing them.

One of X's key principles is 10x thinking. The philosophy is that it's just as challenging to achieve a tenfold improvement as it is a one-time improvement, so why not aim for the 10x? This mindset is truly transformative.

During our round table discussion with Astro, he posed the question, "What would 10x thinking look like for a sales rep?" This got us thinking about the average productivity of an enterprise sales rep, which is around a million dollars. What if one rep could generate $10 million or even $100 million? Was there a way to achieve this?

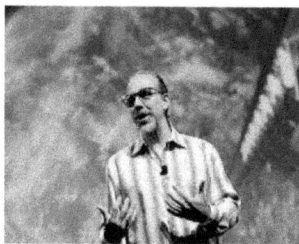

Astro challenged us to think 10x in Sales

This thought-provoking exercise led us to innovate how we built our sales team. The same approach can be applied to other sales or team projects. What is the moonshot? What is the big idea you and your team could pursue?

Innovation is a Team Sport

One of the things I found cool about X was that they would assemble groups of people from diverse backgrounds to work on projects. They might have an engineer, a designer, and a woodworker all collaborating on a project because they would see things differently and provide varied perspectives. I particularly appreciate this approach because one of my favorite movies is *Ocean's 11*. I enjoy watching diverse individuals come together to pull off a job successfully. In the movie, you have someone skilled in explosives, a technologist con man, a circus performer, and people from various backgrounds collaborating to create a heist—a remarkable project.

At X, we implemented a similar approach with our team. We had a diverse group of individuals from different backgrounds. Notably, we had someone on the sales team who was also a development engineer, which helped us develop better sales systems. It was one of the best and most successful teams I've ever led.

When building your team, include people from diverse backgrounds, experiences, and capabilities. You will find that you get better results.

X invited thought leaders from all backgrounds to foster innovative thinking. Some notable individuals included Kim Scott and Leonard Susskind (Quantum Physics).

Make Contact with the Real World as Fast as You Can

Prototype of the driverless car at X

If someone has a brilliant idea, create a culture that encourages them to build a Mininum Viable Product as quickly as possible. Teams often spend too much time discussing plans and never actually build anything. A prime example of this is Google Glass. In the former visitor area, there are examples of early models created at X. Google Glass's first iteration was a pair of Ray-Ban sunglasses with a camera attached and custom software written to work with it. This illustrates the culture of "If you have an idea, build something quickly." I still hold this belief today. When someone on my team has a great idea, I ask them to create a prototype as quickly as possible. This allows us to see if it works in practice and saves time if it doesn't, enabling us to fail quickly and learn from our mistakes.

Give Back to Others

While X was a demanding environment, it also created a culture of giving back to others and improving the world. They encouraged their employees to spread the message of innovation to diverse groups. This allowed me to work with a non-profit organization dedicated to education (Think Together), which provides after-school programs to those who may not have every opportunity to succeed.

One of the best days of my career

I hosted five young people, giving them a tour of X and showing them how we operated. They saw drones, robots and balloons. We had a "question and answer" session, and their imaginations ran wild with the possibilities of what they could do. We then shared lunch at the marketplace. I hope these five youngsters will never forget their experience.

I also consulted with a non-profit organization about their sales process. I met with their team in a series of off-site meetings and taught them some of the sales techniques and processes we used at X. They implemented these strategies. A few years later, after I had moved on, I received an email from one of the board members informing me that the non-profit's contributions had more than doubled since they had implemented the lessons learned while we worked together at X.

X supported all this work; it is part of their culture of giving back and making the world a better place. These experiences also made me a better leader and were inspiring opportunities for our team.

Study the User and Build Your Product Based on Their Job

When we first developed Project Lantern, we were assigned a design team trained to study how people perform their jobs, document their findings, and provide us with insights. This allowed us to comprehend how individuals carried out their tasks and how we could best support them with the technology we were creating. The individuals conducting the study were not necessarily technical experts but came from backgrounds that enabled them to analyze processes and human behaviors. They applied their expertise across various projects, technologies, and concepts. We then leveraged the information obtained from the study to guide the development of our product. I firmly believe that the product was greatly enhanced because we took the time to understand how people performed their jobs and then tailored the product and software to accommodate and improve their work experience. This approach proved to be a significant success with our customers.

Use Spaces that Encourage Collaboration

X is an old shopping mall that has been converted into offices. I use the word "office" lightly because nobody really has any private offices in X. Everyone works out in the open, and when meetings are required, there are meeting rooms available.

What I noticed and learned to appreciate about X was that all the spaces they created for collaboration were furnished with couches, bean bags, comfortable chairs, round tables, and all sorts of different places where you could get together as a team. They also encouraged eating together.

While there is always the legend of the free meals offered at Google, X's approach created an opportunity for collaboration. It was rare for someone to eat alone at X. You would often meet a new person or collaborate with your team.

Inside of X

These comfortable spaces made a significant difference to our team. We had something we called "the couch," which was an old couch in our area. Our team often took their laptops and worked from there, which became a great source of collaboration and creativity.

Have Some Fun While You're Doing It

When our team started at X, we had five people on our go-to-market team. It was one of the best teams I've worked with. We were asked to provide an overview of our team and our go-to-market plan to the senior people at X.

X has a culture of fun and play, which contributes to their creativity. One of our team members had a one-eyed French bulldog named Reggie. Google is a dog-friendly company, so the team member often brought Reggie to the office. He would sit in our conference rooms during planning sessions and walk around to everyone to get a pet. During meetings, he would often be in the corner of the room, snoring. He became a mascot for our team.

So, when it came time to present our team and org chart, I created an org chart that showed all the team members with their pictures and titles and a picture of Reggie, the one-eyed Frenchie, listed as our team mascot. I also listed myself as the chief bottle washer for the team.

While it was a small thing, it became a cultural moment for the team we were building because it demonstrated that while we took our work seriously, we were also having a good time.

Have a Burrito Story

When we initiated the project that eventually became Chronicle, our founder, Mike "Chainsaw" Wiacek, had a narrative that resonated profoundly with the company and market. We fondly refer to it as the "burrito story." One day, while working at Google, he was sitting in a room, savoring a burrito, when a group of executives entered, discussing a severe security breach that had impacted the company. Intrigued by their conversation, our founder intervened, suggesting it might be a nation-state attack. His astute observation surprised the executives, prompting an investigation that ultimately uncovered the Aurora attacks—Chinese attempts to hack into Google and other tech giants. This revelation laid the groundwork for Google's TAG (Threat Analysis Group).

This incident served as the primary inspiration for the product we developed at Chronicle. It imbued our company with a profound sense of purpose, encapsulating how, why, and for what we stood. Through my experiences, I've realized that startups need their version of a "burrito

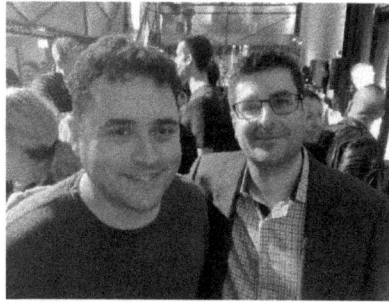

Our co-founders "Chainsaw" and Shapor were the soul of Chronicle

story." It emotionally connects the market to the company's inception and mission.

Fail Fast and Celebrate It

The process at X is designed to create moonshots. One of their strategies is to attempt to kill a project at every stage of its life cycle. Expert committees are tasked with identifying reasons why a project will not succeed, such as potential pitfalls or failure mechanisms. Initially, I perceived this approach as overly negative. However, I came to realize its positive impact, as it allowed the team to address and resolve potential problems before project failure.

I applied a similar mindset to our sales team. I began to evaluate deals by identifying potential obstacles and weaknesses. The team could address these issues and enhance the likelihood of closing the deal by doing so. I emphasized to my team that my role was to "Kill the Deal"—critically assess deals and identify potential issues. This approach allowed the team to address these issues before jeopardizing the deal's success.

We Are All Human Beings and Have Lives Beyond Work

Leading a team during COVID could have been one of the hardest times of my career. There wasn't a guidebook on how to lead people through a pandemic. You had to figure it out as you went along.

One of the things I learned was about our shared humanity. People were taking Zoom calls from their bedrooms, living rooms, and kitchens. I remember having forecast calls with my head of operations, who had his beautiful little baby daughter on his lap while he took care of her, and we discussed the forecast with a group of people during the call. I also recall kids running in the middle of our calls and saying hello.

I remember when people were sick and fearful for their lives. I also remember the friends and family who died during the pandemic and how difficult it was for people. Sometimes, during calls, people, including me, would break out and start crying because of all the pressure we were under and how scared we were.

I always knew we were and saw us as human beings at work, but this experience truly showed me what I call our "shared humanity." There is no such thing as work-life balance. Who we are at work and who we are outside of work should be the same person. We must recognize that we are all human.

I am much more forgiving now of people and their situations. I want to know those personal situations and try to support people. I don't think business will ever be the same after what we learned through the pandemic. We're not robots; we have hearts, dreams, emotions, families, friends, and faiths.

Recognize Your Humanity: Moments of Humanity

When I first started in business, the leaders I saw were always the tough, unemotional, unflappable types. Sure, they were human beings and showed their humanity—but not really. They often wore masks and only showed what they thought was required of how a leader behaves. I learned that as well. It wasn't until COVID-19 that I had to learn about other people's humanity and my humanity.

There was one time when I was under tremendous personal pressure because my mother was very ill. I was on a forecast call in front of a large group of people, and I snapped. Somebody reduced their forecast and gave me a surprise, which I hate. I then raised my voice with this person and showed my disappointment in front of a group of people. It was not a good moment.

During the rest of the meeting, I felt guilty and thought about how that was not how I wanted to behave. So, toward the end of the meeting, I stopped it. First, I apologized to the person I snapped at in front of everyone. Then, I spoke to the team. I said, "Folks, you just saw my humanity. I'm under a lot of pressure personally, and I let it get out, and I should never do that. I'm very sorry you saw this, and I hope you know that I'm not proud of it and that what you saw was my humanity as well. I hope that I can be patient with all of you when you have these human moments." The person accepted my apology.

After the meeting, I received a Slack message from one of the people who attended that call. He said he had been in the cybersecurity industry for twenty-five years and had never seen a chief revenue officer apologize like I did. Most chief revenue officers would have yelled and screamed and thought nothing about it.

Life is too short not to accept your humanity. We make mistakes. As leaders, we have personal pressures, and nothing puts more pressure on us than COVID did. Acknowledge your mistakes, apologize for them, and use them as teaching moments.

Be Kind to Others and to Yourself

When I was early in my career, I detested when people made excuses. I believed that you should do whatever it takes to make things happen—that was how leaders operated.

During the COVID-19 pandemic, I learned many valuable lessons about humanity. One of the most important lessons was the importance of kindness. Showing empathy, listening to others, understanding that people have lives outside of work, and demonstrating compassion can make a significant difference.

Tenacity - Never, Never, Never Give Up - Be Visible

I have always admired Churchill's leadership. I have read many books about him and his leadership, especially during World War II. When we were going through the pandemic and acquisition at Google, it was tumultuous, to say the least. The employees were unhappy with the situation, which was a test of my leadership and ability to keep people together.

I went back and studied Churchill and how he led through World War II. When he took over for Neville Chamberlain,

Great Britain was in a dire situation, and the Nazis were close to overrunning Europe. The British needed to know their mission and for what they stood. Churchill assumed the mantle of leadership and famously declared, "We shall never surrender." He said they would fight all the way to the end, and he would, too. It was a powerful statement that rallied the British people behind him and gave them strength as the Nazis relentlessly bombed them.

It made me think about how I was leading the team at Chronicle. I made it clear to the team that we would never give up. We would see it though and do our best to stay together as one team. Churchill's leadership inspired and supported me through a difficult time with our

MOTHERBOARD
TECH BY VICE

'Chronicle Is Dead and Google Killed It'

Chronicle, Google's moonshot cybersecurity startup that was supposed to completely change the industry, is imploding.

team, which tested my leadership skills. Ultimately, we were able to get through that challenging situation and deliver great results. The business has continued to succeed since my departure.

2

Building a Championship Sales Organization

It Takes Time to Build a Championship Team

I tend to be a very impatient person. (I'm still working on this.) When I take over a team, I want to start winning and being successful as soon as possible. I've taken great comfort in leaders like Bill Walsh and Dawn Staley; both have built amazing programs: Bill Walsh with the San Francisco 49ers and Dawn Staley with the University of South Carolina Women's Basketball team. I've studied both of those leaders and what's interesting is that they both had losing records in their first two years of coaching. It really taught me that it takes time to build a program and that it doesn't happen overnight.

2–14–0 record

In 1979 Walsh returned to the NFL as head coach of the San Francisco 49ers. The team struggled to a **2–14–0** record in his first season but by 1981 had emerged as NFL champions with a victory in Super Bowl XVI. Nov 29, 2022

14

You start by building the culture and bringing on the people who will implement the system, but it takes time. Learning this taught me to have patience in how I build a program. I don't believe in overnight success or that things can turn on a dime. If you want to build an enduring program, it takes time.

Make Sure the Task is Clear

One of the observations I've made about joining new teams is that the sales organization's task is often unclear. One would think this would be a minimum standard in any organization. I recall joining a company where there were three numbers: the board's number, the field's number, and an aspirational number, and they were mixing them all up.

I like to ensure the task is completely clear and agreed upon going into it. What is the *one number* we're all publicly striving for? It doesn't mean you don't have a different number for the board, and it doesn't mean you don't have aspirational numbers. However, when you face the field and the organization, there should only be one number that everyone is working toward. I've found that this clarity of task creates focus and energy within your organization.

Be Intentional; You Set the Pace

In one of my previous leadership roles, I encountered a team with a culture characterized by excessive drinking and partying. I recognized that this culture was not conducive to success and did not align with the values of a championship team.

To address this, I decided to set the standard myself. Public actions are among the most effective ways to communicate a cultural shift. During the sales kickoff event, which traditionally involved late-night partying, I consciously decided to break away from this norm.

Instead of joining the late-night festivities, I opted to be in the gym at 6:00 a.m., setting an example of dedication and professionalism. Surprisingly, I found some others who shared my commitment to early morning workouts.

Sales Kickoff 6am Workout Club

During my opening address at the kickoff, I acknowledged and celebrated these individuals, recognizing their hard work and dedication. This simple act had a significant impact on the team's culture. The following day, the number of attendees at the gym increased to around twenty-five, and this became a regular feature of future kickoffs.

I explained to the team that the old administration's approach ended the day at 6:00 a.m., while the new administration would start the day at 6:00 a.m. This symbolized our commitment to excellence, professionalism, and being the best in our field.

The result of this cultural shift was remarkable. Over the next three years, our team was recognized as one of the best-selling teams in American Business, a testament to the power of positive culture and leadership.

I continued this practice with my managers. Before each sales kickoff, I would hold a mini workshop with them to discuss how they wanted to be perceived as a management team by our people. This open dialogue allowed us to set clear standards and expectations for our behavior during the conference and beyond.

By being intentional about how we presented ourselves, we created a culture of professionalism and excellence that contributed to our team's success.

One Team, One Mission: The Victory Plan

One of the most frustrating things for a salesforce is not having a clear attack plan. The salesforce needs to know how to get an A and how to be successful. Top-down plans never work in my experience. It should always be a combination of a top-down and a bottom-up plan. Therefore, I always use what's called a Victory Plan. It's a one-page business plan that takes the task assigned to the sales team, typically the bookings target, and breaks it down into thirteen to fifteen goals with the associated measurements. If you achieve the goals, you will deliver the task back to the business, which is your booking target. The team must build this plan. You can't build it yourself and hand it to them. The truth is in the field, and the best ideas are always in the room.

Before the beginning of every year, I facilitate a meeting where my direct reports and other supporting department representatives get together and create a plan in four key areas: business results, customer satisfaction, employee engagement, and operational excellence. These are the goals and associated measurements that we will focus on executing, regularly assigning them a red, yellow, or green status. When there's a red status, we focus the team on improving or fixing that red area. It all fits into one plan where you share the results with your team, providing transparency. Everyone knows where they stand, and there is no confusion about performance. It creates focus, accountability, and transparency within the team. I have even used my Victory Plans as recruiting tools because most teams don't have a plan that is simple and clear.

Dr. Martin Luther King Jr. has provided us with many valuable lessons on leadership. One lesson that has significantly impacted me is his emphasis on doing one's job to the best of their ability and taking pride in it. He famously said: "If you're going to be a street sweeper, be the Michelangelo of street sweepers." This quote resonates deeply with me, as I believe it highlights the importance of pride in our work and connecting people to the significance of their contributions. I want everyone on our team to understand that their role, whether it be as an unsung contributor supporting the sales team or as a high-profile sales representative, is crucial to our success. Regardless of my position, I share this sentiment. I strive to excel in whatever task I undertake.

Which is the most important (business results, customer satisfaction, employee engagement, or operational excellence)?

In the Victory Plan, there are four key areas where we set business goals. I remember having a meeting with twenty-five of my frontline managers to create a Victory Plan. It was a great experience. It was challenging to get a team like this to create a plan.

A manager once asked which of the four areas was most important. Business results typically contain new pipeline logos and targets aligned with the business's health. Every manager in the room except one said business results were the most important category.

It was a courageous moment. He raised his hand and said, "I think employee engagement is the most important." He had started his career as a server at a restaurant where the employees were treated incredibly well. Managers were trained to treat their people well. As a result, the restaurant chain was very successful and had high customer satisfaction.

His point was that if you have inspired, motivated, and well-cared-for employees, they will take care of your customers and deliver the results. It was an incredible moment because when he finished speaking, every manager in the room agreed with him, and we all agreed that employee engagement was the most important of all the goals.

If you have great people who are treated well, trained, and inspired, they will serve your customers and drive success in your business.

The JT Posse

When the new chief revenue officer started at Gartner, and I was his Chief of Staff, I noticed he had a group of consultants who helped him run his program. At the time, I didn't understand why he needed them, and I thought he was just taking care of people who had been in his network for a while. However, I've learned that with each new company, it's invaluable to have people who have worked with you before to help you build it. These consultants know me and have experience working with me to build programs. Syd Kain at Kain and Colosanto has helped us recruit and build

Sales Teams. Nicky Baumohl at Evolutionary Events helps us deliver the world's top sales events. Jay Tyler at JTC leads our management and high potential training. Chad Sanderson at Value Selling Associates implements Value Selling with our sellers. Many of these people have been with me for over twenty years. These are all people who have helped me implement my program quickly. I call them "The JT Posse." I couldn't build a great program without them.

Have a Framework for Making Decisions and Communicate it to Your Team

As a C-level executive, your words carry a lot of power. I recall a story I was once told about an executive who walked into a factory, looked at a wall, and said, "I wonder what that wall would look like if it were blue." Months later, he returned to the factory and saw that the wall was indeed blue. He asked why they had painted it blue, and the person replied, "Well, you said you wondered what the wall would look like if it were blue, so we painted it blue." The executive responded, "That's not what I wanted."

I learned from this story that when you think aloud, people often interpret your thoughts as decisions. The best way to counteract this is to have a framework for your decisions and communicate it to your team, peers, and direct reports. Show them how you make decisions, explain when you have made a decision, and clarify when the decision is final. Don't leave it ambiguous; don't think aloud without giving your team a criterion for determining whether it's a decision. They want the certainty of knowing when you've made a decision and when that decision is final.

Run Key Plays

I have always believed that running plays is a smart strategy. I learned this valuable lesson when I played basketball. The teams I played for emphasized discipline in their plays. This approach proved highly effective, as it allowed us to operate as a predictable team, delivering consistent results. It was also incredibly helpful when the pressure mounted, as we didn't have to think as much since we knew exactly where we needed to be and what we needed to do. Often, this would overwhelm and break down the opposing team.

I have discovered that the same principle applies to sales, particularly at Chronicle. We were unsure how the market would respond when we launched our product. We had some initial ideas based on feedback from our first customers. To address this uncertainty, we created four key plays within the revenue triangle, which encompasses product, marketing, and sales. These plays would guide our sales team's actions, covering every aspect of the sales process, from the initial contact with a prospect to the final closing of the deal. The plays included specific questions to ask, presentations to deliver, and proof-of-concept demonstrations. Essentially, they provided everything a sales representative needed to know to successfully execute the play and convert a prospect into a customer.

One of the interesting aspects of these plays was that there was one we didn't initially think would be the most effective, but we wanted to test it to see what would happen. Over time, we discovered that this play became the one our prospects preferred to run most often. This unexpected finding prompted us to revisit our product and engineering teams to make necessary changes to the product to meet the market's demands.

In contrast, there was another play, for which we had high hopes, but it was not well-received in the market and wasn't generating a new pipeline. Creating these four key plays allowed us to identify what was working and what wasn't, enabling us to make timely adjustments. Moreover, it provided a consistent framework for engaging with our prospects in the marketplace.

The Sales Leader Playbook

I believe you win or lose based on the success of your frontline sales leaders. As I often say, a frontline sales leader's role is the hardest job in a company. Frontline sales leaders have constant requests for information and demands coming down on them, and they are responsible for what goes on in the marketplace with their sales representatives. It is a challenging job.

One of the things I like to do is create a sales leader playbook for myself and the entire organization of managers. We all follow one playbook to run the business. The playbook aligns with the Victory Plan's four key areas: business results, customer satisfaction, employee engagement, and operational excellence. It outlines what we should all be doing as sales managers, from reporting on business performance to coaching in the field, hiring people, and running the business.

Staff Versus Field

When I build a team, I talk to them about the relationship between the field and the staff. I believe both roles are distinct and critical. The staff typically comprises my head of sales operations, finance, and HR. They are responsible for ensuring the field has the right plan, resources, and tools to win. My field leaders are responsible for delivering results. They are sales, channel, and engineering leaders who face the market daily. Both are critical to success, and neither ranks above the other on my team.

I am fascinated by history, and one of its greatest stories is the Normandy invasion in World War II. The invasion's success was mind-boggling, considering the logistics that had to be coordinated. While generals like Montgomery, Patton, and Bradley received accolades for their success in the field and ultimately in the invasion, they would not have been successful without the logistics support provided by people like Walter Bedell Smith and others who ensured they landed on the right parts of the beach with the right equipment, tools, and support to be successful.

How To Get an A

In my experience, everyone strives for excellence, symbolized by the coveted "A" grade. However, many teams fail to provide clarity on achieving this goal. My approach is to cascade our Victory Plan throughout the team and furnish every team member with a document titled "How To Get an A." This document outlines the eight to ten essential actions anyone in their role should take to succeed. It's based on field input and insights from successful reps.

To gather these insights, I engage with our top reps and inquire about their consistent practices that contribute to their annual success. We then codify this information and share it with all our employees, ensuring they clearly understand how to achieve an "A." Additionally, we measure their progress toward this goal. When every team member comprehends how to get an "A" and aligns their efforts with the success of the Victory Plan, team success is virtually guaranteed.

Unfortunately, I've observed that many teams suffer from unclear expectations and goals, leaving employees uncertain about how to excel. My approach aims to eliminate this ambiguity and empower everyone to contribute effectively to the company's success.

Get Your Team Rowing in One Direction: The 3x5

I prioritize creating clarity and focus for myself and my team. To this end, I have implemented a weekly meeting routine. Every Monday and Friday, we gather for thirty to forty-five minutes to utilize what I call the 3x5 document. This document captures the three critical tasks each team member will execute during the following five days. Each team member contributes their three items, and we review them as a team at the beginning of the week. At the end of the week, we assess our progress on those tasks using a simple red, yellow, or green rating, indicating whether we achieved them or not. Ensuring alignment with our Victory Plan is crucial.

By implementing this 3x5 document process, I have observed several benefits. First, team members often discover that they are working on similar tasks, which presents opportunities for collaboration. Second, duplication of efforts becomes apparent, preventing multiple team members from undertaking the same task simultaneously. Furthermore, the process builds collaboration and mutual support within the team. It is not uncommon for someone working on a task to receive valuable insights or assistance from another team member. By incorporating the 3x5 document and regular check-ins, I have effectively streamlined our workflow, encouraged teamwork, and maintained a clear focus on our objectives.

The Dreaded One-on-One

In my experience, most one-on-one meetings tend to be unproductive. Neither party is prepared, and the conversation often revolves around superficial questions like, "How is everything going?" This approach is inefficient and ineffective in ensuring alignment and addressing critical issues. To address this, I prefer to treat one-on-one meetings as sacred time. During these meetings, I inform my team that they have my undivided attention and can discuss any items or issues they wish. I extend the same courtesy to my manager.

I manage these meetings using a template inspired by a technique taught to me by a mentor. The template consists of four main areas:

1. Current Issues: What are the current issues I need to be aware of?
2. Request for Assistance: Where do you need my help?
3. Company Updates: What are the latest company updates?
4. Action Items: What action items have we taken that need follow up?

The simplicity of this template allows us to focus the meeting on the most important matters. I prioritize one-on-one meetings with my team and manager and rarely skip them.

By employing this template, I've found that conversations are more focused and structured, enabling me to effectively accomplish my objectives with my team and manager. Additionally, it allows my team members to communicate and batch-process items they want to discuss with me throughout the week, making it an efficient use of time.

One of the luckiest moments of my career was meeting Dick Boucher.

One of my mentors, Dick Boucher, whom I affectionately refer to as "Grizzly," introduced me to this technique during a meeting in his living room. As we discussed how to improve meeting effectiveness, he excused himself to his home office and returned with a typed memo. He handed it to me, explaining that it was an example of a one-on-one document he had used in the past. Remarkably, it was a one-on-one document between him and Andy Grove, the CEO of Intel. It contained notes and was closely aligned with the format we had discussed for running one-on-one meetings. Recognizing the value of this approach, I adopted it for my meetings, believing that if it was good enough for Andy Grove, it was good enough for me.

Forecast Versus Pipeline Review Meetings

Forecast meetings and pipeline meetings should be two separate events. A forecast meeting is for me as the manager to understand what the rep is doing, their prediction for the business, and their forecast. Typically, reps don't get much value out of this, and it's mostly for the manager to understand what's happening in the business. A pipeline meeting is for the rep and the manager. This is an opportunity for them to review their deals, demand gen efforts, and determine if they have enough pipeline to achieve their goals. It's an opportunity for the manager to coach and help the rep succeed.

When those two meetings are combined, they invariably end up being a forecast review and a grilling session rather than a value to the rep. So, whether you set them up as two separate meetings or divide the meeting into two, there should be a distinct separation between a forecast review and a pipeline review.

Words You Should Never Use in a Forecast Meeting

There are certain words I never use or allow my leaders to use when talking about a forecast or pipeline. Words like "I hope," "I think," and "maybe" are words that say you don't know what's going on or what's happening. Also, I always speak using the active voice instead of the passive voice, and I expect my leaders to do the same. That means every sentence has a subject, a verb, and an object. It sounds silly, but words matter. Saying words and using phrases like this on a forecast or pipeline call indicates to the people that you don't know what you're doing. If you don't know, say it. If you don't know, find the answer. Your strong language speaks in the active tense and never uses words like think, hope, or maybe. They will just make you sound weak and unpredictable.

You Win or Lose with Your Frontline Managers

Frontline sales leadership is one of the most challenging jobs in a company. Pressure cascades from the "ivory tower" in the form of priorities, reports, and meetings, which rain down on a sales manager. Sales representatives hunger for coaching, support, advice, and counseling. Customers, prospects, and partners all have demands.

Your frontline managers ensure all the requests and demands are fulfilled. They must believe in you as their chief revenue officer and trust you have their best interests at heart. They should feel emotionally connected to you and be willing to go the extra mile for you. Second-line managers are too far from the action to drive the business effectively.

Managers Versus Leaders

The term "leadership" is frequently used today, becoming a diluted concept. However, being a leader and a manager are distinct roles. Before becoming a leader, one must learn to be an exceptional manager.

A sales manager plays various roles, including coach and counselor, sales strategist, chief inspiration officer, and talent magnet. Mastering these four areas is crucial for successfully leading a team of salespeople. Salespeople rely on their managers to excel in these areas; otherwise, the manager's role becomes redundant.

Once a manager demonstrates proficiency in these areas, they can instill belief, create a vision, and exhibit other characteristics of a good leader. It is essential to differentiate between the roles of a manager and a leader, as words do matter.

The PACK Method for Sales Compensation Plans

Sales compensation plans are fundamental to any successful sales organization. It's often said that what you pay for is what you get. If sales representatives scrutinize the compensation plan to identify loopholes, gaps, and opportunities to make money, they will. I often say that if you gave ten sales reps the United States' Federal budget as a compensation plan, they would likely fix it within a week. Sales reps are adept at taking advantage of compensation plans.

Over time, I've developed a methodology for creating compensation plans that I call the PACK methodology.

P stands for pay for performance. Reps should receive a commensurate amount of money for great performance. I want reps to feel like they can win the lottery. Therefore, I don't favor capped plans.

A stands for aligned. The plan should align with the company's strategic plan and desired outcomes.

C stands for consistent. The plan should be consistent among all employees in the organization. Creating one-off plans is a nightmare for everyone and leads to uneven results.

K stands for keep it simple. Sales leaders often want to create complex plans to drive every desired behavior from reps. However, in my experience, the simpler the plan, the easier it is to manage, and reps can easily know how much money they can make.

My philosophy is that a rep should know exactly how much money they'll make when they go on a sales call and create an opportunity in their pipeline. I want a direct connection between their actions and the money they'll make. The more complicated the plan, the more opportunities for reps to find loopholes.

I once had a complicated compensation plan as a manager. I found a loophole that allowed me to make a windfall if I drove a small amount of business in addition to my regular responsibilities. I took advantage of the loophole and made a lot of money, and they had to change the plan.

Your Central Command Center: The Control Book

Early in my sales management career, I created a control book. It was a document that showed me our top deals' current forecast or pipeline and what was happening in the business. It was a very simple document, but it gave me a solid view of the business.

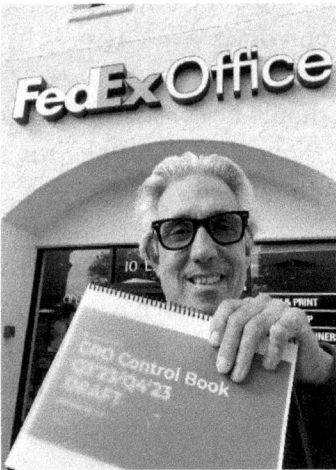

Getting a new control book!

Over time, I have continued to use this control book. It typically includes sales rep activity, demand gen performance, pipeline MRI (a deep dive into the pipeline), current and next two quarter forecast, headcount, sales rep productivity and capacity, pricing, key plays, and win/loss. It's comprehensive but allows me to focus on the key parts of the business and understand the trends and what's happening. I typically like to have electronic and hard copy versions because I take notes when I question or inspect the business. Also, I like to keep previous control books so I can go back to my notes and see what's changed and whether people did what they said they would do.

This system has worked very well for me because it allows me to see all areas of the business, connect them, and form my own opinions. I still use technology like Clari and Salesforce to help me predict the business. However, as I have said before, as a sales leader, you have to get to the "source data" and "connect the dots," which means you must dive into several different sources of data and connect them to see what's happening in the business and predict future trends.

Playing Scramble with Tiger Woods

Early in my management career, I encountered a term called "participation." When I first heard it, I wondered what the leadership team meant by it. I learned that it was the number of representatives on a team who were on track to achieve their quotas. This was viewed as a health indicator of the business.

Later, I heard a concept that applies in sales: "playing scramble with Tiger Woods." In golf, a scramble is a type of tournament where four people play together. They take their shots, but they always play the best ball of the best player in the foursome. At the time, Tiger Woods was the number one golfer in the world, and someone remarked that a particular sales team was "playing scramble with Tiger Woods."

I asked what he meant by that, and he explained that only one person on that sales manager's team was overachieving their quota, and it was masking the underperformance of the others on the team. Essentially, it was a team relying on one person to deliver results while everyone else was failing.

To this day, I like to assess team participation with each of my teams. If you have a team where every representative is making their quota, it's a rare and challenging feat—one that I have only accomplished a couple of times in my career. It's a testament to the health of a team when everyone is achieving their targets. You have multiple ways to win, and it's likely a team that feels like it's succeeding.

On the other hand, if you have a team where only one person is making their quota, and the managers are also making their quotas, you only have one way to win, and it's likely a toxic culture.

The Plan To Crush the Plan

I enjoy having plans, especially documented ones. As the chief revenue officer, my team and I have developed the Victory Plan. I want every sales representative to have a territory plan and act as if they were the owners of their own businesses. To facilitate this, I encourage them to create an annual "plan to crush the plan." This ten to eleven-slide document serves as a template that guides reps through their business, opportunities, and goals, enabling them to formulate a plan to surpass their targets for the year.

During my time at Google X, one of the co-founders, an engineer by profession, posed a question to me: "JT, why do you need a 'plan to crush the plan'? Isn't it just a plan?" It was a valid question. The primary reason for naming it as such was to instill a psychology and mentality within the salesforce to consistently exceed their goals. I wanted my reps to think beyond merely meeting their quotas and to strive for exceptional performance.

A remarkable experience at Google reinforced the effectiveness of this approach. One of our European sales representatives diligently followed the "plan to crush the plan" process. As a former professional tennis player, he possessed the discipline required to execute such a plan. He set ambitious goals and outlined a detailed strategy to achieve them over the next twelve months. Although his targets appeared aggressive, his work ethic and intelligence gave me confidence in his ability to succeed.

After leaving the company, I was astonished to receive a message from the same sales rep early the following year. He had exceeded all his sales targets, achieving over 200 percent of his quota. His performance was extraordinary. He attributed his success to the plan he had crafted, which he executed diligently. He emphasized that setting such audacious goals was crucial in driving his exceptional sales performance.

The Field CTO

I've always believed sales engineers are a vital element in sales. As I've often said, I've never sold anything without the assistance of a sales engineer. This became even more apparent during my time leading the Symantec technical sales organization. I witnessed their incredible impact on prospects, customers, and partners when selecting Symantec products. I began referring to them as "field chief technical officers" or "field CTOs." They truly appreciated the respect and responsibility this title conveyed.

This concept came to fruition at Google when my Field CTO—one of the most exceptional sales engineering leaders I've ever worked with—helped us build what was arguably the best team of sales engineers with whom I've had the pleasure of working. Their success was largely due to her ability to assemble a talented group of individuals who possessed a remarkable combination of business and technical acumen.

Many of them came from engineering backgrounds and had the remarkable ability to dive into code and start writing effortlessly. However, they were also skilled at articulating the value of our products to technical buyers.

I recall a specific meeting with the owner of a significant partner of ours. He inquired about the technical future of our product. My field CTO was seated beside me, and I jokingly remarked that while my lips would be moving, he would hear her voice.

I unconditionally rely on my field CTO to guide the technical direction of our sales organization and shape how we operate in the market. While we shared a laugh, it was an essential point to make.

I was particularly proud of this field CTO because, in a male-dominated industry, she stood out as a female leader. She remains one of the most talented technical leaders I've had the privilege of working with.

What I Look for in a Sales Rep: The Four Legs of a Table

There are four characteristics that I look for in a sales representative. I call them the four legs of a table.

Leg #1: Traits. Traits include curiosity, competitiveness, teamwork, intellectual horsepower, grit, willingness to overcome adversity, ability to set and achieve goals, and having a goal orientation.

Leg #2: Sales acumen. This is a portable sales process and a way that you manage your business, showing you can repeat it at my company.

Leg #3: Business acumen. I want the candidate to know how a business operates and how businesspeople and executives think.

Leg #4: Technology acumen. They should not only be comfortable using technology but also be comfortable selling technology. They should understand how technology works and how it makes their business better and be open-minded.

If a candidate has strong legs in all four areas, I have a great candidate. Traits are non-negotiable for me. You have to have that leg. A table will still stand a little wobbly with three legs, so if one of the other legs is a little weaker, that can often be improved through a great program, training, and enablement, and through great traits. Four legs are the best, but for high-potential candidates with strong capabilities in other areas, I would potentially hire them without all four being strong. However, they're not a good candidate for me if they don't have at least three legs, including traits.

The Four Roles of a Sales Manager

The sales manager job is the hardest job in a company. They coach and manage their reps and spend time with customers, prospects, and partners. They also have to manage all that's coming to them from headquarters. These could be forecasts, pipelines, or requests for product capabilities. The list of what a sales manager has to deal with goes on and on.

With all that in mind, there are four key roles of a sales manager:

Role #1: Coach and counselor. You have to be someone who can coach and counsel your group of sales reps. Being a sales rep is a difficult, emotional job with a lot of pressure. Being able to coach and teach your reps is critical.

For instance, the most important point for coaching a sales rep is during a sales call. Attending a call with the rep and giving feedback on how they conducted the call is an important coaching role for a sales manager.

Role #2: Superior sales strategist. To provide value and earn respect with your team, you must understand how a deal gets done and help your sales reps get things done, whether with their prospects or within the company. You must be someone who can help strategize with a rep to help them progress toward their goals.

An example is when a sales rep is working on a complex sales opportunity. They should be able to count on their sales manager to give them sales advice about managing the opportunity and assisting with navigating the internal company people necessary to win the deal.

Role #3: Chief inspiration officer. They have to create an esprit de corps within their team and inspire each team member. It's a tall order and requires that a manager knows what's in the heart of each of their people and sets the situation up accordingly. It's not just about numbers. It has to be about hearts and minds.

For example, a manager should know what is in the heart of each of their team members: What inspires them? What demotivates them? What is their why? Then, they must keep all that in mind as they manage the person. Salespeople often tell me they want to make a lot of money. This triggers a series of questions. "How much is a lot of money to you?" Often, I find that reps think too small when they think about what a lot of money is. The point of being a sales rep is that you can make an extraordinary amount of money if you drive an extraordinary performance. I ask, "What would you do with the money if you had it?" I want to know what tangible thing they will do with the money. For example, is it to buy a house, a nice car, or put their kids through college? Then, I ask the most important question: "What would it mean to you if you could do this?" This gets to the heart of what it means to them and what they will do to achieve it.

Role #4: Talent magnet. A great frontline sales leader attracts, retains, and develops great talent. They have to always be on the lookout for new reps and talent. They also have to be able to spot talent and develop it to achieve their targets and for future opportunities.

Top managers are always looking for talent. They typically have a "talent bench" of people with whom they have built relationships (internally and externally) and would be replacements if a team member left or if their team expanded.

Salespeople: The True Warriors in the Arena

I have immense empathy for salespeople. Typically, 50 percent of a sales rep's income is at risk. They must sell to earn enough to support themselves and their families and live a decent life. It's the most accountable role in any company. A sales rep usually has 365 days to meet their quota. Therefore, every day matters.

I often hear sales leaders say that time is the most important asset for a rep, yet they don't provide the rep with their territory, quota, or compensation plan until thirty or even ninety days after the year starts. This is a disservice to the reps. My goal has always been to give the rep their quota, comp plans, and targets on the first day of the year, if possible. It gives them the most time to achieve their goals.

Additionally, I've observed that managers waste reps' time with useless meetings and reports, pulling them out of the field and taking away from their ability to hit their targets. The only objective that matters to a rep is achieving or exceeding their target; that's why they do the job. Respecting their time, providing them with what they need to succeed as quickly as possible, and removing barriers are the marks of a great sales leader.

I often say during internal meetings where sales reps are present, "I will make this meeting quick, as there is no one on this call buying our product today." It's a lighthearted way of saying that I respect their time and don't want to waste it on internal meetings.

One of my favorite speeches is the one Theodore Roosevelt gave at the University of Sorbonne in Paris. It's a remarkable speech, and the part that has resonated with me for years is the talk about the man in the arena. Today, we can talk about the person in the arena. What I like about it is how relatable it is to sales and being a sales rep. A sales rep takes a quota. If they make it, they make money. If they don't, about half their income is at risk. To me, this is the ultimate being in the arena. They put their money where their mouth is.

I have great respect for salespeople and the craft of selling. That's why I get annoyed when critics give them a hard time. Most of those critics don't have their money at stake like sales reps do. Most staff people, supporting actors, and people sitting in the arena can make close to 100 percent of their targeted income by showing up every day. Most sales reps can't do this. They are truly on the arena floor, fighting against the competition, trying to find opportunities and close them.

Sales Calls: The Pre-Call Plan and "The Debrief"

Depending on the segment a rep sells to, some reps may not have more than one sales call per week, while others may have five to seven sales calls per week. Each sales call should be treated as a valuable interaction with a prospect, customer, or partner. Pre-call preparation is essential, where everyone involved understands their role, who will control the call, and the objectives of the call. Executives who prefer to improvise are disrespectful to salespeople. All attendees should be fully prepared before attending a meeting. In my experience, a sales call never unfolds exactly as expected. Still, preparation is key to ensuring confidence during the call and addressing unexpected twists and turns that inevitably occur.

With that in mind, it is a disservice to the rep if you do not debrief after the call. I make it a priority to debrief after every sales call, following the same process each time. I asked the rep about the call's objectives and how we performed. We discuss the three things that went well and the three things we could have improved upon, and we outline our next steps. I seek feedback from each person who participated in the sales call.

In my experience, reps tend to be overly critical of themselves, so it is important to prompt them to identify the positive aspects of the call. Allowing them to provide feedback before offering your own is crucial. The goal is to teach reps to be reflective and self-aware about how a call unfolds. While you have your observations about what went well and what didn't, you want the reps to recognize and understand these points on their own. Therefore, everyone else provides their feedback first. After summarizing their input, I offer feedback, focusing on one or two things that went particularly well and one or two areas for improvement. I provide general feedback about the call as well.

It is important to approach the debrief as a coaching opportunity, not just a critique. The goal is to guide and teach the rep so they can enhance their skills and improve their performance.

Where a Sales Manager Should Spend Their Time

I remember when I first became a sales manager, sitting at my desk at 11:30 at night with the fluorescent lights overhead, going through an endless list of action items, meetings, and things I had to follow up on, wondering what I was doing. Over time, I learned that one of the hardest things about being a frontline sales manager is that everyone demands your time. What you say no to is as important as what you say yes to.

Therefore, I developed a field management process outlining where to spend my time. I began by designating how much time I wanted to spend in the field, typically 40 to 50 percent. Then, I allocated time for one-on-one meetings, team meetings, quarterly business reviews, administrative tasks, recruiting, and field time. I scheduled these activities in blocks on my calendar. Doing this gave me better control over my day and allowed me to focus on what was most important.

Getting Everyone into the Boat: The Cross-Function Business Review

Silos arise when individuals become engrossed in their work and lose sight of the broader impact on other teams. Silos often occur unknowingly, with sales and customer success teams commonly being the most affected. Those are the teams that are responsible for making sure that everybody gets together to serve the customer or the prospect. Ultimately, customers and prospects are the most affected by silos.

I've implemented cross-functional accountability through cross-functional reviews. During these reviews, I invite members from customer success, services, support, legal, finance, and product to join the meeting. This ensures everyone is taking responsibility for their deals.

For instance, if customers are dissatisfied with the product and I'm unable to make additional sales, the best approach is to have everyone involved provide a red, yellow, or green rating for each customer. This gives the sales team visibility into areas where we can assist customers in achieving "green" status while providing the customer success and support teams with insight into areas where customers are struggling and new deals or sales may be blocked.

No one enjoys having a red or yellow label next to their name or being held accountable for a negative outcome. Therefore, I schedule regular calls that everyone is expected to attend. During these calls, we review yellow and red ratings and hold each other accountable. This builds teamwork and collaboration, as it's not an accusatory meeting but an opportunity for everyone to work together toward a common goal.

It's important for me to be more critical of my direct reports than those who don't report directly to me, as this demonstrates teamwork and sets an example for others to follow.

Enterprise Sales Reps: Love To Win Versus Hate To Lose

I am naturally a "love to win" type of leader. A "love to win" leader thinks anything is possible. They set ambitious targets and lead people through hope, optimism, drive, and planning.

My favorite type of enterprise sales managers and reps are "hate to lose" people. These are people who detest losing. They pay attention to every detail and are always worried about missing something. They tend to have a healthy dose of paranoia and are always thinking about why things might not go as planned. This is an important mindset when managing sales opportunities.

Often, sales reps will live on "Hope Island." They hope the deal will close and things will work out. The best enterprise sales managers are the ones who consider all the reasons why a deal might not happen. They are paranoid and think they might have missed a detail. As I like to say to one of my sales leaders, "I sleep soundly at night knowing they are awake sweating the details."

Forecast Versus Best Case Versus Pipeline

Sales managers must know how to categorize deals in the pipeline and leverage that information to forecast business outcomes. I want to clarify the definition of a "forecast deal" or "commit." To me, there's no such thing as a "blood forecast." It's a term I've heard sales leaders use, which essentially means basing forecasts on a commitment that's like pulling teeth. I find that unreliable and believe it puts undue pressure on sales managers, often leading to poor decisions driven by fear.

I want my managers to forecast based on the sales process, stage definitions, and their experience in the field meeting with prospects. I expect them to be within a margin of plus or minus 10 percent of their forecast. I understand if they forecast below their quota. Another bad behavior is when sales managers tell their teams they must forecast their quota. This leads to missed forecasts and sudden drops at the end of the quarter as managers artificially inflate their numbers.

I prefer managers to call the business as they see it. If they're below quota, they should submit a gap plan explaining how they'll close that gap and then work to execute it. This creates a culture of accountability, visibility, and truth in the team.

Additionally, I want them to use their best-case scenario to give me an idea of how much potential they have in the pipeline. This indicates how much they could add to their forecast if things go well with the deals in their pipeline. The earlier stage deals in the pipeline are typically worked within the quarter but don't have a high probability of closing during that time.

My goal is to build a team where managers accurately predict business performance. We work together to bridge the gap if it falls short of quarterly expectations.

Regarding forecasting, I believe in triangulation—a methodology popularized by Bill Clinton. Triangulation involves gathering and combining data from multiple sources to form a comprehensive outlook. I leverage data from the Control Book, manager and rep inputs, weighted averages, and personal observations gained from field visits. This approach allows me to consider various perspectives and make informed decisions.

I aim to be a "beat and raise leader" who consistently delivers accurate forecasts, strives to exceed expectations, and maintains predictability. This can be challenging, especially when forecasting below the quota, but it's crucial for building credibility with senior leadership.

Predictability is paramount, as it enables effective resource allocation and decision-making. Starting with an unrealistic quota and later lowering it damages credibility and undermines trust. Therefore, I prioritize setting achievable targets and developing a clear path to reach them. Your boss will be much more forgiving if you forecast below your quota and achieve it versus forecasting at or above your quota and missing it. A rule of thumb is that I like to see sales managers at plus or minus 10 percent of their forecast at the beginning of a quarter.

I worked with one sales leader who consistently missed his forecast. He was a good sales leader, but he was overly optimistic. I told him he lived on "Hope Island." His forecast was based more on hopefulness that things would happen versus using cold, hard data to predict what would happen. Ultimately, he had to leave the company because we lost confidence in his ability to forecast.

By embracing triangulation and focusing on predictability, I strive to deliver reliable forecasts that guide the business toward success.

Forecasting Below Quota Should Trigger the Words "Gap Plan"

While I do not pressure my team to forecast their quota, the words "gap plan" immediately come to mind whenever they forecast below their quota. A gap plan is a plan created by the manager or the rep that outlines how they will bridge the gap between their forecast and their quota. It includes specific actions they will take to ensure they achieve their quota. I appreciate this approach because it places the responsibility back on the manager or rep to own their target. Sales managers who yell, cajole, or pressure reps to forecast their target essentially take ownership of the forecast as much as the rep does. I prefer to keep the responsibility in their hands, where they must find a way to close the gap and take accountability for any shortfall.

Fight Until the End: It's Not Over Until It's Over

One of the things I love about sales is that it's never over until it's over. A sales rep or team always has until the last minute of the year to make their quota. I often say the world ends December 31 at 11:59:59. This mindset is crucial, as it drives an unwavering determination to fight until the very last second, recognizing that anything is possible. Numerous stories exemplify this relentless spirit, where sales reps and teams have pulled off remarkable feats at the proverbial eleventh hour.

One such instance occurred during my time as a sales rep at Gartner in my first full year. I had worked diligently to build my business and was in a solid position. However, with just thirty days remaining in the year, I still needed to close a significant deal to achieve my ultimate goal: earning the prestigious Eagle Award, earned by the top 1 percent of sales reps. Despite the looming deadline, I remained focused and persistent, continuing to work, drive meetings, and pursue every opportunity.

Then, out of the blue, the phone rang. It was a prospect I had been nurturing throughout the year, informing me that a new executive had joined their team and expressed interest in establishing a new business relationship within the next thirty days. It was a major opportunity that emerged at a critical juncture. I dedicated all my time and effort to this prospect, assembling a team to support our efforts. As fate would have it, we transformed a customer who had previously spent $80,000 with us into one that generated well over a million dollars. This pivotal deal catapulted me over the finish line, securing the coveted Eagle Award. Had I succumbed to despair with only thirty days left, this extraordinary outcome would never have materialized. It was a testament to the cumulative effect of all the hard work and perseverance I had invested throughout the year, which culminated in those final thirty days.

Another remarkable example involves a sales rep I had the privilege of managing. After serving in the military in Afghanistan, he joined our company with just six months left in the fiscal year. Despite his late start, he set ambitious goals for himself, aiming to surpass his quota. His relentless focus on activity was truly exceptional, as he consistently scheduled a multitude of prospect meetings every week. He meticulously built a robust pipeline, yet by September, he had only achieved 1 percent of his quota. Despite the seemingly daunting odds, he never wavered in his belief in himself. A significant breakthrough came in the form of a challenging deal we closed in September, which opened the floodgates for him. All the groundwork he had laid, the persistent activity, and the unwavering effort paid off, culminating in a remarkable achievement on the last day of the year. He closed the final deal, securing his position as the world's number-one sales rep. It was a performance that left me in awe. He would never have attained such extraordinary success if he had given up when he was at 1 percent of quota in September with four months still ahead. To this day, I cherish the photograph of him receiving the award for being the top rep in the world. Moments like these make my heart soar, and I will forever treasure the memory.

Another memorable instance occurred toward the end of the year at a previous company. Besides software, we also sold hardware. A unique aspect of hardware sales is that revenue recognition can only occur once the product has been physically shipped to the customer. On December 31, we had one last deal that had to ship to meet our target. The head of sales operations went above and beyond, taking his wife to the airport at LaGuardia, where he inspected and watched the equipment being loaded onto the airplane. He even sent me a picture of the shipment around 10:00 that night, with him and his wife beaming in the background. That single deal propelled us to our target, making it a truly unforgettable moment.

The team fought all the way to end and made it

The final and probably most memorable event of all occurred at Chronicle. GCP had just acquired us, and the media announced that the "Chronicle was dead." Despite this, the team remained committed to the plan, stayed together, and fought until the very end to achieve our Victory Plan. We made our plan on the night of the last day of the year, December 31, by 1 percent. It was the most remarkable performance I've ever witnessed from a team.

With Compensation Plans, I want the Reps To Think They'll Win the Lottery

I'm a big believer in Maslow's hierarchy. I want to connect the commission and payment for closing a deal as closely as possible to the moment the deal is closed. I aim to create a strong association in the rep's mind that they will receive a reward when they close a deal. With that in mind, I like to create a vision where reps believe they can earn unlimited money by selling our product. I call it encouraging reps to think they will win the lottery.

In my experience, very few reps actually "win the lottery," although I have seen reps make up to a million dollars in commission checks. What happens is that this potential becomes advertising for the rest of the organization, where everyone dreams of making significant money for outstanding performances. I believe this builds a high-performance culture where people strive for greatness because they know they can win the lottery.

Sales Achiever Club is Not Your Vacation

The Sales Achiever Club, often known as the President's Club, is an opportunity to recognize sales reps and their key supporters who have achieved their quotas or played a crucial role in helping others achieve theirs. It's typically held at a luxurious resort and serves as an additional reward for sales reps who meet their targets. It's also a great way to build camaraderie within the organization. Typically, spouses and guests are invited, making it one of the most important times of the year for me.

This event is not only a chance to recognize top performers but also an opportunity to acknowledge the people who supported them throughout the year. I have a runbook for this event that details everything, including photos and names of attendees and their guests. I study these so that when I'm at the event, I can introduce myself to the guests and let them know how much I appreciate their support and effort.

Additionally, I do everything I can to serve the attendees and make them feel special for their contributions. When my management team and I attend a Sales Achiever Club, it's not a vacation but a work event where we care for our people. The goal is to create an experience so rewarding that your team and their guests never want to miss a club event.

Have a Repeatable Sales Process and Stick to It

When discussing sales methodologies, the first thing I empha-size is to pick one and stick to it. Ensure everyone, from the chief revenue officer to your sales reps and SDRs, consistently uses the chosen methodology. I typically focus on two parts of a methodology:

1. **How you engage with prospects, customers, and partners:** This often involves a methodology like value selling, where you use a questioning and strategic process to work collaboratively with your prospect to create a solution. This approach is typically used in more solution-oriented sales.

2. **The sales process:** While related, this is separate from the engagement methodology. A sales process is about understanding where you are in the deal; it's a roadmap with defined stages. Methodologies like MEDDIC and others function as sales processes. I've developed my own sales process called the 5x5, with five stages and five steps that align with the Victory Plan process.

Whatever you choose, pick one and use it consistently. If you don't know where you are in the stages of your sales, it's very difficult to predict your business. In my experience, sales methodologies and stages are often rolled out as optional exercises for most sales teams. I make it a point to ensure the sales methodology is practical for the field and helps us accurately predict where we are in a sales opportunity.

Direct Sales Are Not the Only Way To Win

Direct sales are not the only way to succeed in the marketplace. You must meet customers and prospects in the market where they want to buy. One of the ways they'll want to buy is through partners.

There are multiple ways a B2B tech company can work with partners. This can range from value-added resellers, distributors, value-added distributors, system integrators, and services partners. The list goes on and on.

The way I lead channel leaders is similar to how I lead direct sales leaders. I like giving them a quota and discrete accountability for the business, even if they're working with the sales force. I also expect a channel leader to think strategically.

More is not better; selecting the right partners with the right business proposition is critical. It also matters what types of partners you pick because some will deliver short-term results, like a value-added distributor or a services partner, and others will take years to develop, like a technology partner or system integrator.

A great channel leader should have a strategy for all the different ways of going to market and the timing to go to market. At Google, we were fortunate to have a fantastic partner leader who built a long-term strategy for how we went to market with our partners. She executed it flawlessly, becoming one of the most significant growth drivers for the business.

Reduce, Reuse, and Recycle

Creating new PowerPoint decks every time someone asks a question can be a significant waste of time. Instead, I prefer to create a core set of slides and decks that I can reuse in different presentations. I call it "Reduce, Reuse, and Recycle." This means we should have a set of the most important slides and data that are essential for the sales organization. We should reuse them for sales kickoffs, quarterly business reviews, peer reviews, and board meetings whenever possible. "Recycle" means using a similar format for quarterly all-hands calls, team meetings, peer reviews, and board meetings. The more consistency you have in your decks, the data you use, and how you present, the more comfortable people will be with the data you're presenting and the more predictable you'll become.

So, if someone asks me a question requiring data, I typically like my team to first look at the current data, review the existing slides, and see if we can reuse what we've already created. I've found this approach saves time and creates consistency.

Leading Versus Lagging Indicators

In my experience, sales leaders often focus on lagging indicators. What are lagging indicators? Things like closed business and short-term forecasts are lagging indicators based on past activities that you can't significantly impact or change. I prefer to focus on leading indicators. What are leading indicators? Leading indicators are all sales rep activity, meetings, proposals, longer-term pipeline, leads that match your ideal customer profile, new rep productivity, and ramp times. These can give you insights into the future of the business and enable you to make decisions that can positively impact outcomes.

Focusing on lagging indicators doesn't drive better results. Focusing on leading indicators is more challenging because there's so much pressure to deliver short-term results, but if you don't, you'll never get ahead and will ultimately face problems down the road.

I once read a book that stuck with me. It was about how to set up an organization, and the author compared it to running a factory. He emphasized the importance of understanding the process in your organization and identifying potential bottlenecks. This concept also applies to sales. Selling is like a factory process. It often starts well before anyone speaks to a sales rep—when a prospect visits your website, attends a webinar, or looks at the content your team has created. These are engagement points that must be monitored.

In my experience, a leader will typically miss their target before they even realize it. If I'm in the first quarter of the year, I should be closely examining the second half of our business to see if we have enough pipeline and if sufficient new pipeline is being added to achieve our targets based on close rates. This is critical if your business has an enterprise or mid market segment because the sales cycle is often 180 days or longer. So, when I talk to a chief revenue officer, one of the first questions I ask is, "What does your second half look like, and how much new pipeline is being added?"

A Great Business Review

I vividly recall a quarterly business review during my early years as a sales manager. It was an intimidating experience. Imagine walking into a room with a rigid template, facing a group of critical individuals eager to challenge you with unpredictable questions. The process felt valueless and time-consuming.

One incident stands out. A presenter was under such relentless questioning that they started sweating profusely and eventually fainted during the presentation. Someone joked the old phrase, "Down goes Frazier," which only became amusing after we confirmed the person was alright.

Determined to improve the experience, I transformed the business review process when I led my team. I envisioned the rep as the customer and structured the meetings accordingly. I provided reps with a template to outline their business plans and current status. Assigned panelists listened attentively without interruptions. Afterward, each panelist posed questions or offered recommendations and assistance to the rep.

The impact was significant. One rep remarked that it was the first meeting of its kind in their career and that they had never felt more supported by the team. The process pressured panelists to engage actively, provide feedback, and take action items from the reps. Reps appreciated the support and genuinely wanted to help them grow their business.

Sometimes, You Need a Do-Over

In college basketball, my coach emphasized the importance of respecting the game. Whenever the team performed poorly or lacked motivation in practice, he would dismiss us from the gym, telling us we didn't deserve the privilege of playing basketball. This served as a wake-up call, reminding us of our love for the game.

As a team leader, I've encountered similar situations in business reviews. When a senior person fails to take the process seriously, I sometimes intervene by halting the review and requesting a do-over. This can be a bold approach, but it often serves as a wake-up call, motivating the individual to come back stronger.

A similar approach can be effective when teams are learning new skills. While at Google X, I observed a team struggling to collaborate effectively on a business review. After their presentation, I provided feedback and requested a do-over by Monday. Initially shocked, the team rallied together and delivered an impressive presentation on Monday, demonstrating teamwork and alignment. This experience became legendary within our team, emphasizing the importance of teamwork and giving one's best effort.

Sales Kickoffs Have Three Objectives

Sales kickoffs are an expensive use of resources. There's the cost of the kickoff itself, which can run into hundreds of thousands, if not millions, of dollars. Additionally, there's the lost productivity from taking your field team out of the office and away from selling. Therefore, sales kickoffs must efficiently use time and resources. They can't be just a big party or a drunk fest. My sales kickoffs have three main objectives: first, to educate; second, to inspire; and third, to make the team feel part of a culture that's bigger than them. Given the significant investment, I want to optimize every minute of every day. I like to start early in the morning and finish at the end of the day after plenty of work. I make it clear to the organization that this is not just a party; it's an opportunity for us to be educated. By the end of the week, I want the team to feel like they've been shot out of a cannon and excited about the rest of the year.

I've learned that sales kickoffs can be a great opportunity to do very creative things. I like to begin by bringing in a fantastic comedian, like Jake Johannsen, as our master of ceremonies. He typically kicks off the conference with a short monologue, and then between each speaker, he introduces the next one, often adding humorous commentary on the previous speaker. Invariably, he ends up poking fun at all of us executives, reflecting the audience's perspective—and they love it. The executives also enjoy it because it reminds us not to take ourselves too seriously. It's a small touch that makes a big difference in how we engage our organization during sales kickoffs.

Another thing we do is a series of breakout sessions where we teach different classes. One idea we had was to have our managers, executives, and others in the organization teach classes on topics that would benefit sales reps or managers. Sometimes, an executive would talk about how they like to be sold to, while other times, they'd discuss how to give a great business presentation. Top salespeople would teach how they achieved their success.

Jake (pictured with TriNet CEO Burton Goldfield) added an element of fun to our Sales Kickoffs

This approach demonstrates that the truth lies in the field and encourages engagement. Additionally, the people who taught the classes appreciated being recognized for their skills and capabilities.

The Runbook

Leading and running a sales kickoff is a big job with a lot of responsibility, and if not done well, it can be a waste of time. One of the things I like to do is create what's called a runbook. This is essentially a printed guide outlining everything happening at the conference. It includes the agenda, the speakers, the classes being taught, and who is teaching them. I even include pictures of all the attendees so I can study them and remember people's names.

We also provide a smaller version of the runbook to all our executives so they know their responsibilities and what's going on. Additionally, we encourage them to reach out to top performers in the organization to acknowledge their great work and let them know they're available if they need any support. This approach helps ensure the kickoff runs smoothly and effectively.

Rituals with Artifacts

I remember sitting in a meeting, listening to someone review their business. The presenter was an intellectual type who used unique words during his presentations. At one point, he referred to "artifacts"—objects his team used to remind themselves of different concepts. Over time, I've learned that providing an organization with artifacts to remind them of significant moments, themes, campaigns, or teams can make a difference. People tend to be visual and appreciate having objects that symbolize important events or ideas. Museums are filled with thousands of artifacts created over time, and I believe the same concept applies to business.

One artifact that stands out is from our first sales kickoff at Google, when we launched Chronicle. We created a limited number of sweatshirts featuring the Chronicle logo and the theme "Pioneers." We were a group of pioneers launching a new product in a new world, uncertain of what the future held. I still wear that sweatshirt today, and every time I see it, I'm reminded of that kickoff event. Many people from that team still wear those sweatshirts as a reminder of what we accomplished together.

I have many examples of artifacts like this, and they've become special over time. They help create team camaraderie and unity and serve as lasting reminders of shared experiences.

Speedboats

Soon after, we were acquired by the GCP business unit and became the foundational group of its security business unit. I reported to Rob Enslin, the president of sales. He was leading a multi-billion-dollar business, yet he still found time every other week to do a forecast review with me. Given the scale of his larger responsibilities, I often wondered why he was dedicating so much time to us. Once I asked him, "Why are you spending so much time with us?"

He replied, "In my experience if I've ever missed a number, it's always been by millions of dollars, not by hundreds of millions. If I have a small speedboat team like yours that I can count on to deliver millions of dollars every quarter, it gives me more insurance against missing our target with the bigger businesses."

This was a valuable lesson for me in understanding how smaller groups contribute to our overall revenue picture. Sometimes, speedboats save the day.

Brand Your Projects

Branding is a critical element of business. I could go on and on about all the iconic brands that have been created over time. The same is true for organizations and projects. I love giving projects brand names because it helps people remember what they are and creates a mental image, just as brands do. Using names like "Braveheart" for a professional development program or catchy project names based on Greek gods are examples of how branding can be applied to projects. Have fun with it. People tend to remember the brand name. Ultimately, people remember how you make them feel, not just what you told them.

Trade Shows: It's Not About the Booth

Most people in sales and marketing don't understand the hard work involved in managing a tradeshow. They often think that just showing up at a booth and waiting for potential customers to come by is the best use of their time and money. Instead of waiting for people to come to the booth, we take advantage of the event and set up meetings with attendees near our booth or in a separate meeting room. We work the conference not because of the booth but

The TEAM working at the trade show booth.

because of all the relationships we can build within it. We seize the opportunity to meet with people face-to-face when they're outside their offices. This approach allows us to speak with potential customers or partners outside their normal work hours or when they're not working from home, as many people do these days.

The Psychology of Sales

When I talk to people about sales programs we want to implement, I often refer to the psychology of sales. There was a time when I sat in a cubicle with a list of prospects who had no knowledge of my company or what I was selling. My job was to educate them, get them interested, and ultimately convince them to purchase what I was offering. It was a lot of pressure and nerve-wracking because I knew I could be asked to leave if I didn't deliver results within six months. Adding to the pressure was that the VP of sales worked in my office and occasionally left a sticky note on my wall saying, "Have you sold anything yet?" On top of that, my sales results were publicly visible through a monthly sales rep ranking. Worst of all, I couldn't pay my bills if I didn't sell something.

Understanding this psychology of sales and what it's like to be a sales rep is crucial when running a sales team. Factors like clarity of purpose, providing support, making them feel like they could win the lottery, and removing barriers to their success all impact a salesperson's mindset.

I have no real understanding of what it's like to be a software engineer and sit down at a keyboard to write code. Just as there's a psychology to software engineering and other professions, there's a specific psychology to sales.

This is why I don't appreciate "sales hobbyists" or people who think they understand the craft of sales and assume it's simple. It's not.

3

What a Chief Revenue Officer should know

The Average Tenure of a Chief Revenue Officer Is Eighteen Months

People are often surprised when I tell them that the average tenure of a chief revenue officer (CRO) of a B2B software company is only eighteen months. That means CROs don't have much time to deliver results. Typically, they are asked to join a business that needs to grow. It takes about a quarter or two, or six months, to get their program in place and build the business. Then, they have another two quarters to deliver results and demonstrate their capabilities, creating confidence in the CEO and the board. That leaves them only six more months before the end of their eighteen-month tenure. It's a lot of pressure to deliver results in such a short time. As Coach Wooden, the former Basketball coach for UCLA, whose teams won the most College basketball championships would say, "Be quick, but don't hurry." I have a high sense of urgency because I know that, just like a sales rep, a CRO has limited time to demonstrate their performance.

Make the Number

Your number one job as a chief revenue officer is to make your number. As Burton Goldfield once told me, he didn't care whether you overachieved your target as long as you beat it by a dollar. The most important thing is that you always achieve your target. The reason the average tenure of a chief revenue officer is eighteen months is the pressure to achieve quarterly and annual targets. Ultimately, nothing matters more than this. There are many reasons and ways to achieve that number, but never confuse the role of a chief revenue officer with anything other than making sure you hit the number.

Chemistry with the CEO

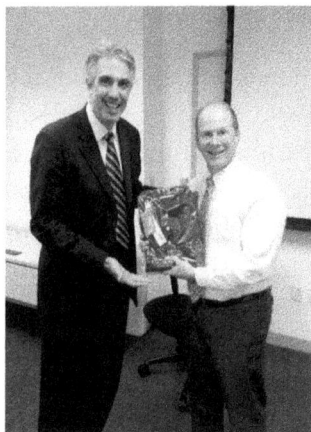

Chemistry with the
CEO is important

I've discovered that good chemistry with your boss and CEO is essential. I never expected them to be my best friends, nor did we need to be friends on a social or personal level. However, I found that a good working relationship, where you deliver bad news promptly, never surprise them, and are there to help solve problems, has made all the difference in my success.

There will be challenging times, and the stronger your collegial relationship with your CEO, the better equipped you'll be to navigate those difficult moments. Chemistry involves shared values, similar perspectives on the world, alignment on team goals, and a spirit of mutual respect.

While there's no confusion about who the boss is, having chemistry makes the job more enjoyable. When considering a company, I always want to meet the CEO as quickly as possible. Usually, within a couple of interactions, I can gauge whether we have chemistry. Do we share values? Do we have complementary temperaments? Will they support my style? Do they not take themselves too seriously? Do they have the maturity and perseverance to work through challenges together? Or are they going to turn against you to save their own skin?

Be Boring

Predictability and transparency are cornerstones of a successful chief revenue officer's career.

Consistency fuels trust: While exciting surprises might have their place, surprising your CEO with unexpected results (good or bad) can create an environment of uncertainty. By communicating openly and consistently, you establish trust and demonstrate your ability to navigate the complexities of the role. Think of yourself as a steady hand at the helm, guiding the ship toward its goals.

Boring is beautiful: As counterintuitive as it may sound, exceeding expectations consistently is more valuable than sporadic bursts of brilliance. Your sales leaders earn your highest praise because you can confidently rely on them to meet their commitments. The same applies to you. When your CEO knows they can depend on you to deliver, it builds a productive and trusting relationship.

Transparency triumphs over surprises: Bad news is inevitable, but hiding it makes things worse. By delivering difficult information promptly and proactively, you demonstrate ownership and accountability. Offer mitigation plans, showcasing your ability to address challenges and find solutions. This open communication strengthens your credibility and earns respect in the long run.

Remember: Predictability doesn't mean stagnation. It's about setting clear goals, communicating effectively, and delivering reliable results.

Do What You Say You Will Do (Don't Overcommit)

As chief revenue officers, everyone wants us to take on more responsibilities. It's easy to come up with new product ideas, sales tactics, or programs. However, executing and seeing things through to completion is challenging. Accepting more than you can handle increases the risk of incomplete tasks.

Similarly, there may be pressure to raise your forecast or push for a higher, unrealistic number. Resist this temptation. When you commit to something, you own it, and others may forget their initial involvement. Ownership entails accountability, so I only commit to what I'm confident I can achieve and aligns with my priorities. Challenging conversations may arise, but ultimately, delivering on promises defines a great leader.

We all face pressure to take on more than we can handle. New ideas are exciting, but execution is the true challenge. Spreading yourself too thin increases the risk of unfinished tasks. Similarly, pressure to inflate numbers can be tempting but don't give in.. When you agree to something, you own it; others may forget their initial involvement. Owning something means accountability, so I only commit to what I can achieve and align with my priorities. Challenging conversations may arise, but ultimately, delivering on promises defines a great leader.

Surround Yourself with Superstars

I'm as good as my team. I've had many teams with great hearts and talent but lacked the skill to do what I needed them to do and what the business needed them to do to succeed. Talent wins. No matter how great a coach or leader you are, it will be challenging or impossible to win if you don't have talent. So, you must always be on the lookout for exceptional talent. When you find it, pursue it aggressively because you will ultimately only be as good as the talent you have, regardless of how great a leader you are.

Build Respectful Relationships with the Board

This was intriguing when I first learned it. When I say build relationships with the board, I don't mean playing golf with them. I'd be just as content if the board didn't know who I was. Board members aim to add value, which can be challenging when you're at arm's length from the business's day-to-day operations. Ultimately, you want board members to know you're competent, have command of your business, and that they can rely on you to deliver on your promises and achieve the results they need the operating team to accomplish. Collegial and friendly relationships never hurt; often, board members can help make connections, reach out to executives, and close deals. I have often said I want to become so competent and reliable that the board barely notices me.

No Line Is ever Linear

When I first started as head of sales, I was having breakfast one day with our chairman of the board, Ray Bingham. We were discussing the business, and I was lamenting how it seemed like we would have a difficult quarter after several quarters of healthy growth. As Ray listened to me, he took a sip of his coffee, looked at me, and said, "John, there's no such thing as a linear line in business. No line goes to the upper right without any interruptions. At some point, you're going to have ups and downs. The key point is how you manage the ups and downs, how you manage the downs, and how you ensure that in the following quarter, the line goes back up. It's more important not to worry about a dip but how you will rectify it over the coming quarters."

I have since learned that any sales leader who says they have never missed a number is either a liar or has never truly been in sales. Every sales leader misses a number sometimes; how they recover from it and get things back on track matters most.

Ride Your Winners

I knew the task would be very difficult during my first hundred days at TriNet. We had to aggressively grow the sales organization, hire many sales reps, and deliver great results quickly. One of the things I noticed is that a group of about fifteen senior sales reps drove most of the company's business. Their productivity had dropped before I started. I wondered why, so I set up an off-site meeting with them to understand the organization's current state and how we could create a future state that would allow the company to grow. We met at the Hyatt in Dallas International Airport, and I invited one of my direct report VPs to help facilitate the meeting.

We sat in the meeting together. It started after lunch at 1:00 p.m. For the next two hours, the team proceeded to vent its frustration about everything happening in the company. I'm usually a pretty good facilitator of meetings, but I wasn't getting anywhere with the group. We called a break, and I went into a separate room with my VP. I told him I thought I couldn't get anywhere with this group and didn't know how we would be successful. He asked to speak with them for a minute before we started again. At that moment, in front of the group, he told them to back off, stop complaining, and work with us to find a way to improve the company.

This pivotal moment marked a shift in the group's attitude as they began to engage and brainstorm solutions for improving the company. The meeting transformed into a productive session where we identified key issues that needed to be addressed. Demonstrating their commitment, the group members volunteered as leaders for each problem, and we collaborated with my peers at the C-level to resolve these issues. In recognition of their exceptional contributions, I named the group the "300 Club," a special milestone in sales at TriNet. We created branded gear and presented it to the group, which they enthusiastically embraced. Over the next six months, the team doubled our growth rate, saving the day. This experience taught me the valuable lesson that sometimes, identifying your best people and providing them with ample resources and incentives can help bridge gaps while building a larger program.

Be an Optimist to My Team; Be a Pessimist to My Boss and the Board

People want to work for optimistic leaders who believe in the future. When I work with my team, I want them to see my optimism, hope, and positive outlook. As sales leaders, we are dealers of hope. Your organization will only be as successful as they believe in you as their leader. So, setting ambitious targets, giving them a vision of what could be, and pushing them to think about stretching themselves is always good.

This is not the approach I take with the board. I'm very conservative with the board and CEO and never over-commit to what the team can do. Often, this will create frustration because the board and executive team want to push you to do more than what's possible. I never deliver good news until I know that the good news is confirmed, and I never seek to please the CEO or the board. I want them to know the real situation, no more or no less.

I remember being in a board meeting where the CEO said we would close the deal. I knew there was no way we would close that deal. The CEO was overcommitting to close the deal and save his job, which was in jeopardy because he wasn't meeting his commitments to the board. A year later, the CEO was no longer with the company.

I'll never forget something General Admiral John Stockdale, a POW and Stanford professor, once said about resilience. He was asked who the people who couldn't survive in a POW camp were. He said the answer is simple. It was the optimists who thought they would be home for Christmas. Once it didn't work out, they gave up hope and failed. Those who survived were realistic optimists. They always believed in the good in the future, but they always had a contingency in their minds that things may not work out the way they wanted.

4

Moving to the CEO's table

You Will Need To Pay Your Dues To Get There

After deciding to leave Symantec and start my venture, I began seeking opportunities. As a first-time VP of sales or chief revenue officer, the best opportunities may not always present themselves. I ended up accepting a challenging assignment at a company that was facing difficulties. I recognized the company's potential for disruption but acknowledged the significant risk involved. The company was based in Long Island, while I resided in San Jose. This required extensive travel, both to the office and in the field. Within a year, I flew over one hundred thousand domestic miles, spending most of it in coach. Balancing my personal and professional lives while proving myself as a sales leader posed significant challenges. Frequent red-eye flights between the west and east coasts became necessary to demonstrate my mettle as a sales leader of an independent company.

One Thursday at 6:00 p.m., I sat in JFK airport, waiting for an inevitably delayed flight home. Tired, exhausted, and lonely, I called a friend who is an accomplished recruiter and has assisted me in building sales organizations. He was walking around in a Staples store, buying office supplies, and contemplated how difficult it must have been for me to sit in that airport that night. Looking back, I am grateful for the opportunity I had. Without paying those dues, I wouldn't have received the opportunities I did and the significant break I got. We now reminisce about that time and laugh, recognizing it as a reminder of the dues one must pay to reach their desired destination. This could also involve undertaking the most challenging project in a company.

Your Peers Are Your First Team

When I first started, I focused more on myself and my team than the company's overall well-being. In retrospect, this revealed me as an amateur who wasn't driving results beyond my organization for the company's benefit. When you are promoted to the CEO's table, you are expected to be an executive team member. This entails building a great sales function and fostering collaboration among your peers to advance the company. The chances of success are minimal if each leader works in their silo.

It can be natural to want to focus on yourself and your team when you join the CEO's table because you want to prove yourself. However, to truly prove yourself as a professional, you must think beyond building a great function to building collaboration among marketing, product, finance, legal, and HR. All constituents are crucial to the success of your function and the company.

One of my favorite books is *Playing the Enemy* about Nelson Mandela and his relationship with the South African rugby team. It is likely one of the greatest human relationship stories I have ever read. Instead of being bitter toward his captors,

Mandela was magnanimous, built relationships, and connected with the people who were imprisoning him. When he was finally released and became Prime Minister, one of the first things he did was build a relationship with the Springboks, the South African rugby team. They were one of the most loved teams in all of

Mandela proved he was the leader for ALL of South Africa

South Africa and represented the white power that had been in power for years. During the World Cup, Mandela went out of his way to build a relationship with their captain and support them through victory. It was a signal that he was the leader for ALL South Africans.

You Serve the CEO

I'm competitive, and when I first started reporting to the CEO, I viewed the relationship as competitive. Sometimes, people would whisper in my ear that I should be the CEO. I didn't want those things to get into my head, but they did.

Over time, I learned that competing with your boss is a foolish idea. Ultimately, you serve at the pleasure of the CEO. They have the power to hire or fire and can either be a supporter or detractor of what you do.

Over time, I've learned that you never want your CEO to fail. You want to help them be successful wherever you can and always support them, whether you agree or not. There should be no competition or any competitive thoughts in your mind. If it is in your mind, it will come across and impede your ability to be successful.

The CFO Relationship: The Schoolyard Fight

One of the things I learned from joining the CEO's table is that when I was a direct report to a chief revenue officer, I often thought the relationship between sales and finance needed to be confrontational. Often, this was because I had short-term goals that needed to be accomplished but were not fully supported by the finance team and were sometimes blocked.

However, I learned at TriNet, by joining the CEO's table and bringing a company public, that one of the most critical relationships was my relationship with the CFO. The CFO and I sat together the last few days of the quarter, working together to ensure we met the target we had committed to the board of directors and Wall Street. My job was to ensure we achieved our sales target, and then I was highly predictable. It was his job to manage expectations from the board and Wall Street. So, the relationship was very tight.

It reminded me of when I was in grammar school, and there would be a big argument in the schoolyard or classroom. The class would split into two sides, and we'd say we'd take it out in the backfield after school. What would then invariably happen is a big circle of kids would be in the playground circling two poor kids facing off against each other, not knowing why.

I felt like that when taking a company public: Everybody wanted to help; everybody was supportive, but at the end of the day, it came down to me and the CFO. I like to say that the CFO and I will not always agree, and we should always have some tension. However, we should put our egos aside and respect each other for the overall good of the business. The company always suffers when the chief revenue officer and CFO are at odds.

Product, Marketing, Sales: The Revenue Triangle

As a sales leader, your relationship with product and marketing will be critical, particularly product marketing. They will help you position and create a pitch, ensuring your team targets the right opportunities with the highest probability of winning. Product is also crucial, as they understand the customers' needs and the needs of the sales force to succeed and ensure engineering builds what you can sell. Sales is obviously important, as we're responsible for driving the company's revenue and bookings.

I like to set up a weekly meeting with product marketing and sales, which I call the revenue triangle meeting. We gather to discuss what's happening in the market, our pipeline, prospects, customers, partners, and how we can improve. It's another critical relationship for the chief revenue officer.

I learned how to create the revenue triangle at Google X. They taught me to have a collaborative spirit and how to build products. We started this regular meeting between the head of product, the head of marketing, and me. We also had a co-founder and our finance person join. We worked through various issues like how to offer the product to customers, price it, position ourselves, and work together to bring on our first customers. It was my first time working so closely with people from cross-functions. We built a creative approach to packaging, pricing, and positioning our product, and it's undoubtedly because all three of us collaborated. It taught me the importance of collaborating with the other two functions. My experience says this applies to early-stage and big companies.

The relationship can also be confrontational when someone lets the other down. Once, a product leader nonchalantly mentioned on a business review call that a product sales were counting on to make its number would be delayed by two quarters. I responded that the product team was "stealing money from the sales reps" because 50 percent of their income is based on what they sell. I made a strong statement, but I wanted the product team to understand that missing targets has implications for everyone, including our customers who were counting on this product launch.

Seeing this type of collaboration carry forward a couple of years later at Google with one of our other teams was fun. We had a product currently in the market that was offered for free—a freemium product. We decided there was the potential to charge for this product if we added more features and capabilities. The product manager, head of engineering, and sales leader collaborated with packaging, positioning, and pricing to bring this product to the market. I remember listening to one of their All Hands calls with their team, including sales engineering and product.. They were presenting a joint plan created with the team they were all collaborating with, and it put a big smile on my face to see them work together as they did. It was one of the most successful products I've seen, growing from $0 to $100 million in revenue within three years.

The CMO Relationship: The Godfather's Undertaker

I can determine whether I'm speaking with a good CMO by asking them one question: "What is your philosophy about the sales and marketing relationship, and how do you judge your success?" The answer is straightforward: helping the sales team achieve its goals. I'm a big fan of marketing, but even with a great marketing team, nothing else matters if the sales team isn't making its numbers.

If marketing wins and sales lose, the company loses. However, if sales win and marketing loses, the company can still be successful. One of the greatest CMOs I've worked with provided an example of this. We faced a challenging second half of the year due to a delayed product roadmap and aggressive targets. Despite a good pipeline, we risked not closing deals. I approached my CMO, requesting his help making the product look as appealing as possible, providing effective messaging, and accelerating the pipeline to facilitate closure in the second half.

I likened it to the scene in *The Godfather* where Sonny is in the morgue. The Godfather asks the Undertaker to do everything in his power to make Sonny look presentable for his mother's funeral. I gave the CMO the same challenge, asking him to make the product look as good as possible until engineering and product could catch up with the roadmap. He promptly went to work, implementing an excellent program with messaging and content. Ultimately, we achieved our goal for the second half of the year. This exemplified the importance of a strong relationship between the chief revenue officer and the CMO.

We agreed that we both owned the sales process up to stage 3 of our 5 stage process. After stage 3, it was up to my team and me to close the business. While I don't consider myself better than anyone else, I believe that sales must win at the end of the day. Great CMOs understand this.

I often say that "all the yelling has been done." This refers to the critical nature of the relationship and the difficulty in achieving alignment. While this process often involves conflict (hence the term "yelling"), strong relationships are built through these conflicts.

HR Isn't the Enemy

Business leaders often perceive HR as an enemy that scrutinizes managers for errors. However, I have a different perspective. My experience at Symantec taught me that an HR business partner can be instrumental in guiding organizational leadership. This partner interviewed all my direct reports and gathered information about the organization, including exit interviews with departed employees, to gain insights into organizational feedback.

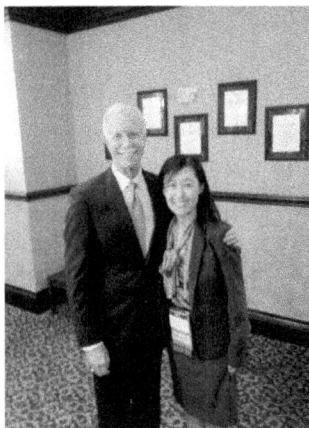

One of the best HR business partners Christine Park with Captain Sullenberger

When I assumed my role, my HR business partner and I met, and she provided me with a comprehensive overview of the organization, significantly reducing my transition period. Over time, we collaborated strategically on talent growth and development within the organization. She played a crucial role in shaping our employees' culture and growth plans.

Since then, I have always ensured my HR business partner actively participates in leading people. Given that people are at the core of my work, my HR leader must work alongside me as a business partner to create an exceptional organization. Junior leaders often view HR professionals as adversaries or enemies. However, it's a two-way street where the HR business partner must be willing to act as a true business partner, comprehending the organization's strategy and deeply involving themselves in its operations.

Not all HR business partners are equipped for this role and may prefer a more tactical relationship. While that's acceptable, they cannot be part of the decision-making process that shapes the organization's future.

Legal and Compliance: Why Does a BMW Go Fast?

While I was working in Europe, BMW was one of our customers. During a discussion with their engineering team, an engineer asked why we believed BMWs could achieve such high speeds. The obvious response was that BMW engineers some of the world's finest engines. The engineer corrected the individual, stating, "A BMW can go so fast because of the brakes. No matter how fast you drive down the Autobahn, you know the car will stop." I considered this a fitting analogy for the relationship between sales and legal/compliance. The chief revenue officer's role is to expand the company as swiftly as possible, while the legal team's responsibility is to ensure the company can brake or decelerate before the chief revenue officer drives the company into a wall. This necessitates open communication among the teams, customers, prospects, and partners for the ultimate benefit. The company will thrive if both entities collaborate effectively, like a BMW.

Know When To Be a Storyteller and When To Just Tell the Facts

I am naturally a storyteller and love both telling and listening to stories. I believe we all enjoy hearing stories. When I joined the CEO table, I often went into storyteller mode during operational reviews and other meetings. I noticed the CEO and some team members were becoming impatient with my storytelling. I sought feedback from one of them, and they told me, "JT, you need to know when to be a storyteller and when to present just the facts and data. When making a case, go straight to the data and let people see it themselves." While I enjoy analyzing and sharing my analysis with others, there are times when you must show the team the data and let them draw their conclusions.

You Want Your Peers To Succeed, and You Want To Be Ranked as the Best Function

I had a zero-sum mentality when I first started at the CEO's table. I believed it was a competition like *The Hunger Games*, where I aimed to be the best function at the expense of others. However, I realized this was a rookie move. Being invited to the CEO's table implies that you are expected to drive the company forward collectively, not just your individual function. This requires collaboration and support among peers to ensure everyone's success. In turn, their role and job is to support you in your sales function. I am competitive and want my function to be recognized as the best by the CEO and the board—but not at the expense of my peers or fellow C-level members at the table.

Using Emotion Versus Data Will Expose You as an Amateur

When I first joined the CEO's table, I used emotion and banged my fist on the table to get my team to do things. Sometimes, it was effective, but most times, it wasn't. Over time, I learned that it was an amateur move, and the fellow executive with the data to support their case would always win the argument.

I eventually learned that data rules the day. When I make a recommendation, point out something that could be improved, or make a point to my peers on the CEO's table, it is always based on utilizing data. When I'm at the table now and see an executive join and try to use emotion to make a decision, they expose themselves as an amateur. Data always rules the day.

Be Three Steps Ahead of the Board

I am not someone who works to please his boss or the board. My job is to understand the goals and targets of the organization and ensure I deliver on them. If I do that, I will have plenty of credibility and appreciation from my boss and the board.

One of the things I've learned about boards is that they really can't get into the operational details of how you run the business. They will never know as much as you do. They may claim they do, but they never will.

I view my job as setting expectations for the board and predictably achieving those expectations. So, when I build a board presentation each quarter, I think about what we're doing today and what we're doing over the next few quarters. Then, I prefer to give breadcrumbs to the board instead of announcing grandiose plans or things ahead of schedule. I want to make sure that whatever I say to the board, I do. This builds credibility and trust with the board. They can only form trust in you based on you doing what you say you will do.

Create a Decision-Making Map

When you sit at the CEO's table, you'll make decisions that impact your peers in other parts of the organization. When I first joined, I often thought about decisions within my work group, which was sales. Later, I learned that some of my decisions upset my peers because they impacted their parts of the business.

What I eventually learned to do was create a mind map. Before making a big decision, I identified all the people who would be impacted by it and those I needed to communicate the decision to, either to get their support or to make them aware of my decision.

You'd be surprised how many people are impacted by decisions made at the CEO table. The more you communicate with your peers and give them a heads-up about upcoming decisions, the better your decisions will be, and the fewer surprises you'll give them. It also builds teamwork.

Nobody Tells You the Truth Anymore

When you join the C-level table, no one tells you the truth again. I say this because people either want to flatter you or make you feel good, and most lack the courage to tell you whether you did a good or bad job. When I give a presentation at a conference or internal meeting, people will almost always say I did a great job; hardly anyone will ever say I didn't do a good job.

I've learned over time to triangulate feedback, take it for what it's worth, and recognize that everyone has a point of view. Very few people will tell you what you did well and what you didn't do well. As an executive, you can't rely on what people tell you or seek their approval. If you do, you'll either be fooled into thinking you're better than you are or be flattered and caught off guard. It's why I use executive coaches to give me feedback. They are paid to tell you the truth.

Understand that when people tell you things, they're probably not telling you the truth or what they really think 90 percent of the time.

The Executive Roundtable

I strive to study and model myself based on the behaviors of successful executives I respect. During my time at Symantec, I had the privilege of being part of John Thompson's organization. I considered him a refined and accomplished executive, a legend in Silicon Valley. Whenever I had the opportunity to be in his presence, I studied him in action.

On one occasion, while I was in Europe, he led an employee roundtable discussion in our Milan office. A large group of people gathered around the conference table, eagerly waiting to hear John's insights. I stood in the corner, closely observing him. He sat in the center of the table, his jacket removed and his sleeves rolled up. He engaged in conversation with the employees, treating them as business partners and sharing his thoughts about the company. His demeanor was composed and calm, creating an atmosphere of casual conversation.

I focused on how he connected with the audience. It was a valuable lesson in conducting roundtable discussions

John Thompson:
a role model executive

effectively. People want to perceive you as authentic and comfortable in your leadership role. I have applied this lesson to my approach when facilitating employee roundtables across various offices and cities. It has been an insightful and valuable

experience developing my executive presence.

You Represent the Company

One of the valuable lessons I learned is that you must appeal to the wider company. If you present yourself solely as a sales leader, you will be perceived as such and not as a powerful, well-respected leader within the organization. Therefore, you must understand the mindset, thoughts, and thinking of your company's various departments and groups. You also need to know how the company operates within sales and the broader organization.

As an ambassador for the leadership team, you should always be prepared to represent the company, not just the sales organization, when interacting with other groups or teams. This will enhance your credibility and power within the company because you will not be viewed as a functional leader but as someone helping lead the business.

Sometimes, Dogs Just Have To Stop and Pee on the Fire Hydrant

When I first started banking, my task was creating credit recommendations for making loans. I worked tirelessly to ensure every detail was covered and I didn't miss anything. However, members of the credit community would often find something or pick on a particular detail in my analysis.

Initially, I wondered why they did this and focused on minute details that didn't make a significant difference. Then, a seasoned professional, "Grizzly," explained it to me. He said executives often want to justify their involvement and show they have actively contributed. They tend to find a minor detail or a trivial point to emphasize their involvement in the process.

Over time, I learned that this behavior is common among executives. They may choose a small, inconsequential detail and focus on it. It's important to recognize that this sometimes happens. Acknowledging their point, appreciating it, considering it, and then moving on is the best approach. Engaging in a big fight over it would misunderstand the real situation.

In one job, I eventually reached a point where I would intentionally include an "Easter egg" in my presentation. It was a minor error that an executive would likely catch and ask me to correct. This would satisfy their desire to identify something incorrect and feel like they had added value to the presentation. I'm not sure if it was the right thing to do, but it was amusing to see how it worked and seemed to satisfy the executives who reviewed my proposals.

If You Break It, You Own It, So Own It

I have learned many lessons from history and biographies. One lesson my operations manager often reminded me of is General Colin Powell's Pottery Barn rule. This rule states that if you buy something and break it, you ultimately own it and cannot return it. It's yours to keep. This rule also applies in business.

Leaders are often asked to temporarily take on additional responsibilities for another department or group. My experience is that these temporary assignments are usually failures. People want to know who their leader is, what the mission is, and what direction they're going, and they want stability. Temporary assignments can be challenging and typically don't succeed.

If you take on additional responsibility for a group or team, own it. Whether you're told you own it or not, you must behave like you own it and be allowed the responsibility to do what you need to do to lead that team successfully. Part-time jobs, acting roles, and temporary roles are typically failures to me. If you take it on, own it, and expect that.

Executives who think they can do two jobs at once fascinate me. Someone might say, "I can be the head of sales, chief revenue officer, and CMO simultaneously," or, "Sure, I can be the CEO and the chief people officer simultaneously." I find it somewhat arrogant to think that you could do a full-time executive job in addition to your job. There's a reason executives are hired and paid what they are. Very few leaders can do two jobs at once.

If you're giving 100 percent in your current executive role, what makes you think you can take on the capacity and add another whole job to your workload? Naturally, there will be some drop-off in your current job and in the new responsibility you take on. You must understand that and build it into your plans.

A Great Consulting Firm Can Help You Go Faster

Earlier in my career, I had an aversion to consultants. My perception was that they often slowed things down, got in the way, and created more work for people. I learned at TriNet and Certinia that working with a good consulting firm can help you accelerate your business because they help you identify the opportunities to improve your business through inspection and their knowledge of the market.

For instance, when I was at one company, our CEO had started a relationship with a consulting firm, the Alexander Group. They did a diagnostic of the sales organization, benchmarked the organization, and made recommendations for improvement. This was an invaluable guidebook for me to use as I came on board and began leading the organization.

I have seen others become defensive and uncooperative with consultants because they see them as a threat. However, working with a consulting firm like the Alexander Group helped us go faster and build a better organization faster.

You Don't Need To Be Everyone's Friend, but You Should Be Collegial

My mentor once told me that familiarity breeds contempt. I thought that was a bit of a harsh statement, but I don't need to be friends with my peers or even my boss. In fact,

I'm usually not socially friendly with my peers or my boss. When we get together for off-site meetings, I enjoy the time and prefer to have a collegial relationship based on mutual respect and enjoyment of working together. My friends and family are separate from my work, and I like to keep it that way. Building friendships and considering your peers and boss as friends can be risky because you may disagree or even have to ask someone to leave the team. Friends don't usually fire each other.

The Chief Revenue Officer Is Always the First Person Killed in the Murder Mystery

I remember watching and reading murder mysteries, and somebody was always the first person killed in the mystery. I believe this person is the chief revenue officer (CRO) in business. There's a reason the average tenure of a CRO is only eighteen months. The CRO role is the most visible and accountable role on the CEO's direct team. It's the only group with a visible scoreboard for evaluating their performance. Your success is determined solely by whether you meet your targets.

The world has changed, and spending at all costs is no longer the way of the world; it's now about driving efficient growth. This makes it even more challenging because you must understand how to get a return from every dollar spent. Most CROs don't have this type of experience.

So, what happens when the CEO or CFO is under pressure? The first person they turn to is the CRO because it's believed that CROs are replaceable and there's an endless supply. This is simply the reality of the job.

Don't take it personally. Run your program, drive results, and know that your job is at risk daily. I find it inspiring to know I'm accountable for my results. I wouldn't want to be someone who isn't ultimately accountable for results. I guess it's because I grew up in a sports environment where you either win or lose; there's no in-between.

Exit Gracefully: The Transition Template

As I have told my team and peers, there are times to board and leave the bus. I envision working at a company and on a project as everyone finding the right seat on the right bus driving toward a destination. At some point, individuals will leave the bus either because they are asked to or because they decide to pursue new opportunities. New people will join the bus and find their seats as you continue toward your destination.

I have always found it best to strive for a graceful exit. To achieve this, I create a transition template that outlines the reasons for my departure, the objectives of my transition, the impact on stakeholders and customers, a day-by-day plan for the transition period, and the potential

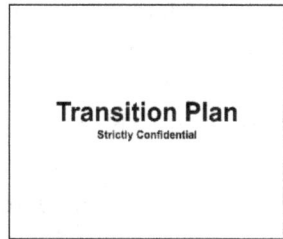

Transition Plan
Strictly Confidential

risks associated with the transition. I have created this template for every role I have left since departing from my position at Symantec in Europe. Controlling the narrative is paramount. Without a unified narrative explaining your departure, people tend to fill the information void with their perspectives. This can be detrimental, disruptive, and counterproductive. I've found executives appreciate my written transition plan. While they may not directly use it, it demonstrates a high level of professionalism in how I intend to gracefully leave the organization. I also share this transition document with my direct reports who are leaving to help them navigate their departures and provide a sense of control over how they exit the company.

Every Project Has a Beginning and an End. When You Leave, Turn the Page to the Next Chapter in Your Book

Sometimes, you leave a company because it's your decision, and sometimes, you leave because it's their decision. I knew an executive who was asked to leave a company, and I noticed that after he left, he continued to contact people there. He remained concerned about what was happening in the company and never seemed to let go. It didn't seem like a good idea for him to continue being connected to the business. It made him appear bitter.

When you leave a job, you should leave it behind. My approach is to turn the page in the book of my life and start a new chapter. This doesn't mean that I don't take calls or contacts from people, but it does mean that I'm not mentally connected to the company anymore. Frankly, other than wishing them well, I don't really care what happens there. I've found that turning the page is better for my psyche and allows me to move on. I believe it also allows the organization to move on.

Nothing positive comes from continuing to meddle in a company once you've left. Move on and focus on your next project.

5

Taking a Company Public

Be Ready For What You Ask For–The Pressure Not To Let the Team Down

Being part of a team that took a company public was one of my career's most exciting and stressful experiences. If you ask my wife, Amy, she would say she never wants me to go through that again. There were days I didn't eat, and the pressure was incredible.

The reason for the pressure was that we had to continue delivering results while going through the initial public offering (IPO) process. There was a lot of pressure to meet sales targets while also ensuring the next three or four quarters post-IPO were in great shape. I felt tremendous pressure because I didn't want to let the team down, and I think our CFO felt the same way.

It's a great experience, but as a Chief Revenue Officer, you are under tremendous pressure to be predictable and deliver consistent results, even when not everything is in your control.

When we finally went public, I was with my sales team at our President's Club in Hawaii. There was tremendous excitement about the IPO. Amy and I flew overnight from Hawaii to New York City to be with the team as we rang the bell on the New York Stock Exchange trading platform. Afterward, we packed our bags and flew back to Hawaii to be with the team.

I knew our future results depended on the sales organization. The truth is always in the field for me. While others attended celebratory dinners and parties to recognize the IPO, as a chief revenue officer, your job just begins once you go public.

If You Become a Section 16 Executive, Everybody Will Know How Much Money You Make

When I was part of the team at TriNet that took the company public, I had no idea what I was getting myself into. The chief legal counsel pulled me aside one day before the IPO and said, "JT, you're going to be a Section 16 executive. I just wanted to let you know." I had no idea what he was talking about and had to figure it out.

It means I'm one of the key people responsible for the company. As a result, my compensation is made public. This means my offer letter, employment letter, income, shares, and how much I have sold are all public records.

Even my sons could look up how much money their dad made on the internet. A few family members contacted me, asking me if they could get a loan. I think some people in my organization looked at how much money I was making and probably thought I wasn't worth it.

It wasn't really that big of a deal, but it was something I had never experienced before and something that you should be aware of if you're considering becoming a Section 16 executive.

Run a Great Business Whether You're Public or Not

Several former CFOs were on TriNet's board. They were all exceptional leaders and highly respected in Silicon Valley. I gained invaluable knowledge from them. I recall one instance when I was having breakfast with one of the board members, and we discussed the distinctions between private and public companies. He emphasized that in today's world, there is no significant difference in how one should manage a public company versus a private one. While compliance rules and additional responsibilities accompany being a publicly traded company, many factors align with simply running a success-ful business. His key message was that if you are operating a predictable, growing, and profitable business, the manage-ment approach should be similar, regardless of whether the company is privately or publicly held. Ultimately, it boils down to sound business practices.

A Strong Investor Makes All the Difference

When we considered taking TriNet public, it was fascinat-ing for me to observe the partner from our lead investor, General Atlantic, guide us through the process. He had a deep understanding of our business and possessed expertise in the workings of public markets. He provided valuable guidance on how to operate the business and what steps we needed to take to become a publicly traded company. We implemented much of the advice given to us. Key relationships were forged through his efforts, and ultimately, we became a successful public company. This experience taught me the invaluable lesson that a great investor can make all the difference in taking a company public.

You Can't Lie to Your Mom and Tell Her You're doing a Great Job if You're Not

I used to tell my team to be careful what they ask for when we take a company public. I would say that when you're a private company, you can tell people you're doing a great job, and they don't know if you're not because they don't know your results. However, when you become a publicly traded company, your results are available for everyone to see. If you do a great job, the stock goes up. If you do a bad job, the stock goes down. There's no hiding. So, as I said to my team, when you go public and become a public company, you can't lie to your mom anymore and tell her you're doing a great job if you're not because she can open the newspaper and immediately see if your company is doing well or not.

Ringing the Bell Is an Event—Not a Destination

I enjoy visualizing my goals. I envisioned myself ringing the bell at an IPO. I cut out a picture of a Chief Revenue Officer who had taken a company public and imagined myself in that picture. I pictured grand parties, recognition, and adulation for our success. However, when TriNet went public, I realized the immense pressure on me and the CFO to deliver results. While the IPO was an exciting and fun experience, especially standing on the New York Stock Exchange floor as our stock was first traded, I felt like I was in the movie *Trading Places*. It dawned on me that the journey had just begun.

As a public company, investors expect you to have at least the next two or three quarters ready to go. This means consistently delivering what you promised to your investors. The pressure to avoid mistakes is significant. Investors scrutinize publicly traded companies during the first few quarters, as it's an opportunity for the company to prove its viability as a public entity.

I tell teams that ringing the bell is great, but it's just a milestone on a longer road. It's an event—not a destination.

6

Attract Winning Diverse Talent

Vulnerability: Attracting Talent is Like a Romantic Relationship

F inding and attracting talented people is challenging. The most skilled people are often successful in their current roles and have many options to consider. Therefore, when I encounter a talented person I believe would be a valuable addition to my team, I make a concerted effort to establish a genuine and personal connection with them. It is imperative for me to convey to them that they are the most important person in my eyes at that moment. Creating a seamless and enjoyable experience is crucial to creating an emotional connection between the candidate, the team, and me. Unfortunately, many people fail to recognize the significance of this approach and treat the recruitment process like a mere transaction.

In contrast, exceptional executives approach recruitment in a manner akin to a romantic relationship. They invest time in understanding what truly matters to the candidate, eliciting an emotional response, demonstrating vulnerability, and creating a sense of exclusivity. Discerning what is important to the candidate and appealing to those values is paramount. For instance, I once encountered a candidate who deeply valued his relationship with his wife and always sought her support before making decisions. Recognizing the importance of this bond, I invited him and his wife to dinner toward the end of the recruitment process. After dinner, I presented the offer letter to the candidate's wife, emphasizing how essential it was for me to ensure their alignment. It was a lighthearted moment, but it conveyed a profound message that they were equally valued and would be integral to our team in their unique capacities. This approach was successful, and the candidate ultimately joined our team.

Moreover, I had the privilege of working with an executive who refused to make an offer until he had met with my wife, Amy. Recognizing the importance of her role in my life, he and his wife invited Amy and me to dinner. This brilliant move created one of the most rewarding working relationships I've ever experienced.

Traits Versus Skills Interviews

There are two types of interviews you should conduct when interviewing a potential sales rep.

One is a skills interview. This is an interview where you evaluate the candidate's ability to run a portable sales process, how they prospect, how they run their business, how they manage their business, and their track record of success. It's a deep interview into how they run their business and will typically include writing on a whiteboard or sharing exactly how they run their business.

The second interview is a traits interview. This is the opportunity to get to know what's in the rep's heart: What adversity have they faced? Where have they been successful.? What motivates them? What demotivates them? What is their why? These questions help you understand if the rep has the traits to succeed in addition to the skills.

I often see people evaluate candidates by mixing these two. However, I treat them as two distinct interviews usually performed by different managers so we can compare notes on traits and skills to get a complete picture of the rep and their potential for success in our program.

I was fortunate to receive an education in high school and college from the Jesuit order of Catholics. This was an order founded by Ignatius of Loyola. One thing I learned when I applied to a business is that businesspeople usually focus on what's in the mind but often neglect what's in people's hearts. I want to know what's in my people's minds *and* hearts. I also want them to know what's in my heart. We are all human beings. We all have hearts, and knowing what's in them makes us better leaders.

At Google, we practiced these traits versus skills interviews. Occasionally, I would be asked to do an interview. One time, I performed a traits interview with a candidate. We got pretty deep into what was in his heart, what motivated him, and why he does what he does. He was a great candidate, and we ultimately hired him. Later, he told me it was one of the hardest interviews he'd ever had, and even his interview for the CIA wasn't as hard or in-depth as the traits interview we did!

When I first became a rep and applied as a sales rep at Gartner, the vice president of the Western US conducted a traits interview with me. I'll never forget the moment he said, "John, I think you're too nice to do this job." He leaned back. I leaned forward aggressively and said, "Of course, I can do this job, and nobody can do it better than me!"

I remember sitting in the parking lot and talking to my wife, Amy, afterward. She asked me how the interview went, and I said I had no idea. I felt numb because I'd never had an interview like that; I'd never interviewed with someone who so deeply wanted to understand who I was and what motivated me.

Equity: Treat People the Way They Want to be Treated

It's important to me to understand my team members' personality traits and preferences. Some people are highly extroverted and will speak at a moment's notice. Others are more introverted and will not speak in a group.

This also applies to diversity. People from different backgrounds behave differently. Some people behave like they're four sit-ups away from a six-pack stomach. They think they know everything and can do anything. Other people are much more skilled and talented than what they know or recognize and are not always willing to raise their hands.

One example of this was a highly extroverted team I led. However, it also included one extremely introverted person. He rarely spoke during meetings. He was self-conscious about his ability to speak English. He was also one of the team's most insightful and brilliant members. After meetings, when everybody had left, I would often send a note to him to ask him what he thought about the meeting and his recommendations. He would typically send me two pages of thoughts, feedback, and ideas about the meeting. His feedback was invaluable. He probably wouldn't have given it to me if I didn't ask him for it. Over time, we learned how to work together, and he would always give me reviews, thoughts, and ideas in a note after meetings. If I hadn't encouraged him to work this way, I would have never received these insights and would not have been as successful.

The same goes for people from different backgrounds. Often, certain people in the group dominate the conversation. As leaders, our job is to look around the table and make sure everybody has a chance to speak. Once, I was in a meeting with a mixture of men and women. During the conversation, the men did all the talking. It just so happened that the women who were in the meeting were the ones who were members of my team. I knew how smart and talented they were. At one point, I stopped the meeting and gave the women on my team room to speak and give their opinions. They were brilliant opinions and moved the conversation forward. Other attendees were confused and somewhat embarrassed, but ultimately, we were better for including everyone's opinions and thoughts.

The lesson is to give your people room to speak, contribute, and be part of the team. Don't assume they'll always be the first to raise their hands.

Assume Positive Intent: "With Love in My Heart"

I realize I make mistakes almost every day in how I treat others. It can be challenging to fully understand other people's backgrounds and sensitivities. I communicate to my team members that my actions and words are motivated by love and kindness. This means assuming positive intentions, which

I also extend to those who work for me. Even when I hear something that could be inadvertently offensive, I choose to assume positive intent. Over time, you can build trust within your organization where people feel comfortable telling you when you've said or done something potentially offensive.

During my time at Google, I often used analogies, particularly those related to sports and war, because I believed they effectively highlighted situations using real-world examples. However, after a meeting, one of my team members discreetly pulled me aside and said, "JT, you need to find new analogies and role models besides sports, war, and men." I was genuinely appreciative of her feedback. I thanked her and reflected on how I could adapt my analogies and role models to the present. This lesson demonstrated her trust in my good intentions and my desire to improve.

Throughout my time at Google, I had many similar experiences where people approached me to explain how certain things I said or did could be delivered more effectively. I was grateful for the trust and faith they showed in me by providing honest feedback.

Always Look for Talent

Attracting and retaining talent is crucial as a leader, as the best teams often have the most skilled individuals.

During a speaking engagement at my alma mater, where I obtained my MBA, an eager attendee who had meticulously taken notes during my presentation approached me. After the event, we engaged in a conversation, and I was impressed by his aspiration to work at Google X and his dedication to preparing for the opportunity.

Despite being a few months away from graduation, I decided to test his seriousness by giving him the task of speaking with my head of technical sales. He passed the tests with flying colors and took the initiative to conduct a project at his university, demonstrating potential security vulnerabilities and how to remediate them.

We extended an offer to him through a rigorous, impromptu process, and he joined our team.

In a memorable incident a few months later, he requested a day off for his graduation, which I gladly approved. I've maintained contact with him throughout his career, and he has since joined the product marketing team at Google, an impressive accomplishment for a recent graduate.

Attending that career session unexpectedly led to discovering an incredibly talented individual, highlighting the importance of building connections and opportunities.

Diversity: I Want *All* the Talent

Diversity is about attracting, welcoming, and retaining great talent. Here's what I learned from a fishing trip in the mountains.

I never went fishing until I had my two sons, Zachary and William. My son William loves to fish, so I learned to love it, too. Once, we were fishing in the mountains of Wyoming with a guide who took us to a fishing lake. The bites were okay but not great. The guide said we'd get better fish if we hiked to the next lake. So, we hiked to the next lake, and the bites were a little better. The guide then told us that if we really wanted great bites and excellent fishing, we'd have to hike another mile on an upward climb—a journey many wouldn't make. We decided to go for it. We hiked up and reached a beautiful, scarcely fished lake. Every time my son cast his line, he caught a fish. It was an incredible experience that made me think about how to attract talent. I want to find talent wherever it exists, even if I have to hike up a mountain.

It's short-sighted for teams to believe they can win by drawing from only half the population—or even less, which often happens when relying predominantly on white males. I want talent from everywhere because it aligns with my value of finding the gold in *all* people.

However, you can't just say you want to attract people from different backgrounds. You have to make the effort to find them—just like hiking up to that mountain lake. Everyone fishes in the same lake, looking for the same people. But it's the leaders who ask for referrals from diverse team members and reach out to diverse communities who find the best talent.

Once you find that talent, you need to create a welcoming environment where those you've attracted feel comfortable and valued within the team. Just as hiking up to that mountain lake was hard work, finding great talent from all backgrounds was hard work. However, I can say that the best teams I've led were also the most diverse.

It's also important to be clear that you're building a team that welcomes people from diverse backgrounds. One of the best ways to build a diverse team is through your existing team members. They usually know who the best people are. When I was at Google X, a female team member said, "JT, it looks like you're really taking diversity seriously. I will give you the names of the three best female leaders I've worked with." I contacted all three, and they were all highly talented. I ended up hiring one of them, who turned out to be one of the best hires I've ever made. She made a massive difference not only to our team's performance but also to our culture.

One of the most gratifying moments in my career was when I left Google. My European team created a farewell video, and what struck me most was the diversity of the people in it. Individuals from different countries with different backgrounds and skills came together in one video to say goodbye. It was a fantastic team because it was composed of talented people from all different backgrounds. Undoubtedly, the team wouldn't have been as successful without its diversity.

Interim Roles

I often see leaders, even at the C-suite level, appoint people to interim roles. In this situation, they give the person responsibility but label it as interim, implying that the person may or may not continue in the role. It is often implied that the person must prove themselves in the job.

I have never liked interim roles because I believe it is a half-hearted decision. Either the person is ready to take on the role or not. Sometimes, I have seen this as a way for leaders to hold back on candidates. They might be less experienced but ready to take on the role, so the leader appoints them as an interim to prove themselves.

My take is that either the person can do the job or they can't. Give them the job and the opportunity to do it, and most importantly, pay and compensate them for the job you're asking them to do. People should not have to prove themselves to get the full-time job or be appointed to the position. A leader should either make the decision or not.

Additionally, people who report to that person in the interim role always wonder whether that person will be permanent or not, which can affect their chances of success.

You Have To Judge Someone's Runway and Push Them as far Down the Runway as You Can

I love developing talent and discovering the hidden potential in people on my team. It's my true passion. When working with someone, I try to determine their growth potential. I call this potential their "runway."

Imagine an airplane with a long runway. It has a great distance to gain speed and momentum before taking off. This allows it to fly much higher and farther than a plane with a short runway.

People are similar. Some individuals have tremendous potential due to their intellectual capacity, work ethic, discipline, and values. These factors indicate that they have a long runway and immense potential.

When I encounter individuals like this, my goal is to provide them with as much support and guidance as possible without overwhelming them. This allows them to continue growing and developing.

One person who worked for me at Google exemplified this principle perfectly. When I first began leading her, she was an inside sales rep. I consistently gave her more responsibilities and provided her with constructive criticism and feedback. She incorporated my feedback into her work and improved significantly as a result. She was promoted four times in just four years, which might be a record.

Her willingness to grow, develop, and work hard determined how far she could go. I have a deep appreciation for individuals with long runways.

When One Door Closes, Two Doors Open

When a decision goes against you, you don't always know if it was the best thing for you. For example, when I was at Symantec, I had been in the role for three years and felt like I was next up for promotion. I was sorely disappointed when someone else was selected for my boss's job. Feeling stuck in my role, I applied for two other jobs but was rejected for both. I was down and disappointed in myself.

Eventually, I decided to leave the company and go to a small startup. I publicly announced my departure, and the chief revenue officer, Tom Kendra, became aware of it and called me into his office. He said, "JT, I don't think you should leave. There's more for you to learn here, and it just so happens I have a big job for you to consider."

Ultimately, it proved to be the job of a lifetime. I moved my family to Europe for three years to learn about how business is done internationally and how to head an organization much larger than the one I was leading in the US.

This experience taught me the lesson that when one door closes, two doors can possibly open. I have maintained this mentality throughout my career, understanding that just because I didn't get what I wanted doesn't mean it was bad. If I had gotten one of those three jobs I applied for, I would have never had the opportunity to go to Europe.

7

Upskilling Your Team

Find the Gold in Everyone

One of the best leaders I've ever worked for told me something that stuck with me ever since. He said, "My job is to find gold in others." When I was early in my career, if I thought somebody was not competent or couldn't contribute to the team, I would write them off as not being useful. This was a limiting behavior and caused me to miss opportunities and great talent.

What I learned from "finding the gold in others" is that it's up to us as leaders to know our people, to get to know their strengths and weaknesses, and to put them in the best situation where they can be the best they possibly can. Everybody wants to do a good job. Everybody has gold in them. It's up to us to find where that gold and hidden greatness is and help them unlock it.

Your Career Is a Mosaic

When I was a kid, I did mosaic art, where I took different pieces of pottery, fabric, magazine articles, and words and used them to make a bigger picture. I always thought it was an interesting way of doing art, and I enjoy seeing mosaics to this day. I have learned that a career is like a mosaic. When I look back at my career and think about where I wanted to be early in my career, there were many things I thought I would need to become the person I wanted to be in the future. I read books, found mentors, took classes, and joined groups to improve myself personally and professionally.

I now look back at all those experiences, which have helped form the mosaic of who I am. For example, people often ask why I'm a good speaker. I spent four years in a Toastmasters group learning how to be a good speaker, lead meetings, and speak on my feet. I'm asked how I know sales and interpersonal skills so well. I took a Dale Carnegie class and was invited back as an instructor. This taught me the basics of interpersonal relationships.

I had many developmental experiences early in my career. They taught me things I thought I might need to become like the executives I wanted to be like.

This is how I coach people for professional development. You don't have to know exactly where you will be in the future, but you should have an idea of what your future looks like in general. Then, you should look at the skills and experiences you have today and the skills and experiences you think you'll need in the future. These could include experiences at work or outside of work, including classes, books, mentorship, and role models. There are many ways to grow and develop yourself and your people.

I continue to see my career as a mosaic and recognize the things I want to keep adding to be the person I want to be in the next twenty-five years.

Everyone Should Have a Development Plan and Keep it Simple

Everyone in your organization should have a development plan. In today's world, one of the most important things to grow, develop, and retain your people is to give them opportunities to grow professionally and personally. I have found that most companies I've been a part of do not have employee development plans. They say they do, but they don't. I know this because when I interview candidates, I ask them if they have a documented professional development plan, and every time, they say they don't. They say they have items they're working on but not a documented plan. The difference between a verbal and a documented plan is that a documented plan provides accountability for the manager and individual contributor to grow and develop themselves.

I use a very simple plan that selects no more than two or three things the person wants to develop and work on. They document them with my coaching. The plans are time-bound and include the activities they will do to grow themselves.

It's also important to schedule a time to review that plan. I've found the best way to do this is to schedule and label it as a "development plan meeting." I like to talk about professional development with people all the time. However, often, if you don't label the meeting as a development plan meeting, people think you're not working with them on their professional development.

So, have a simple documented plan, and at least once a quarter, have a professional development meeting with your people and label the meeting as a development plan meeting.

It's Not a Performance Review; It's a Development Plan

I agree with those who say performance reviews can be a waste of time. If a manager is doing their job effectively, a direct report should always know where they stand and how their performance is evaluated. There should never be any surprises. Weekly one-on-one meetings are an excellent opportunity to provide feedback on employees' performance. It's one of the most important responsibilities of a manager.

Waiting until the annual "grand" performance review to inform employees of their ratings seems like a waste of time to me. The development plan is the most important aspect of performance reviews, to which I devote considerable time.

I created what I called a performance review packet. It included the Victory Plan performance review ratings, a comparison of the employee's performance against those ratings, and an assessment of the team's performance. It also included 360-degree reviews from team members, peers, and direct reports and my assessment of the employee's performance. I also included the management or performance competencies for their job. I wanted to rate them not only on their performance but also on how they were doing in the key competencies of their role. If they were a high potential or ready for promotion, we often reviewed the competencies for their next-level role. Then, we would review a rating process to assess how they compared to those next-level competencies.

In one instance, I reviewed the competency ratings with one of my teammates. The person rated themselves at a certain level. I rated them at a higher level, demonstrating that they should be at the next level. It helped the person understand how to improve themselves, where they were, and when to seek a promotion.

Often, people don't understand what they need to do to get to the next level. This is particularly true for people from diverse backgrounds and genders. Some people are very comfortable asking for a promotion, while others are not. This person was from a diverse background and didn't understand how well they were prepared for the next role. After that meeting, it became clear they should submit themselves for a promotion. I fully supported it, and that person was promoted during the next promotion cycle.

The performance review packet also allowed me to work with the person to identify the three or five things they needed to work on to improve. Performance reviews should always be actionable. They shouldn't be a one-way discussion but an opportunity for the employee to understand how they can improve. That—not the rating—is the value of a performance review.

Use the Moneyball Concept to Build Your Talent

In the movie and book *Moneyball*, the general manager of the Oakland A's baseball team utilized data to identify potential future stars for the team. This was a groundbreaking concept at the time, as most talent scouts relied on instinct to make talent decisions. Consequently, the A's were able to develop future talent that might have otherwise been overlooked.

I adopt a similar approach to building talent within my organization. While I don't rely on data as extensively as the Oakland A's or most professional sports teams today, I prioritize developing and training talent from the beginning to align with our culture. Therefore, I place significant emphasis on entry-level business development rep roles, which are typically filled by individuals early in their careers. These individuals learn to sell our product and understand our company culture. As they demonstrate success, we promote them through the ranks. Many become our top sales reps over time.

We apply the same approach to managers. We conduct a management training class for high-potential individuals to teach them how to manage in our unique way. This training also prepares them for our management culture. Many individuals who have participated in our Moneyball programs have gone on to achieve great things at our company and other companies.

Sometimes, You Have To Take a Short-Term Loss for the Good of the Long-Term Gain

There are times when we are deeply disappointed by something, or a decision goes against us. We then must decide whether to stay on board, fight, or leave the situation. Thinking long term is essential in a situation like this.

Once, when I was a sales manager, I had a compensation plan with a small notice term indicating that achieving a certain target would unlock a significant amount of commissions for me. The management team had not anticipated this small loophole in the compensation plan. I understood it, took advantage of it, and unlocked a large commission windfall.

The commissions were substantial enough to trigger a clause requiring the chief revenue officer to review the commission payment. In his estimation, the payment for what I did was not commensurate with the work. So, they decided to cut my commissions by about $100,000. This was a significant hit, even though I had made a lot of money.

I had a decision to make:

1. Did I believe in the future opportunity of being in that company and my future as a top performer?
2. Or was I going to fight or leave the company based on this decision?

I thought long term and decided to stay on board and accept the decision. The chief revenue officer was grateful for my support of his decision.

Years later, they remembered that decision. I'm sure that impacted the decision to offer me the opportunity of a lifetime to move to Europe and head another organization. It was something I would have never known when I made the decision, but I'm glad I thought about the long term.

I coach people who report to me that when something goes against them that is very serious to them, they must think about both the short term and the long term. Someone who worked for me received a windfall commission that triggered a review by the company's leadership. They ultimately decided to reduce her commissions. I coached her to think about her short-term versus long-term career prospects at the company.

She eventually decided to accept the decision and move forward. It was a great decision. She was ultimately promoted to a role in the enablement organization. She went on to other companies to grow as an executive. Had she made a different decision and either fought or left the company, she might not be where she is today.

It's up to us to coach our people to think not only about the short-term but also about the long-term implications of their decisions.

Feedback Is "The Breakfast of Champions"

A critical aspect of my role involves providing coaching and feedback to individuals. Giving feedback can be challenging, as there's always the risk of using incorrect information or triggering defensiveness. However, top performers often crave feedback to identify areas for improvement. They tend to be hard on themselves and may not recognize their strengths. In contrast, underperforming individuals often resist feedback, preferring to hide and avoid confronting the reality of their performance.

I never pass up an opportunity to provide feedback, whether it's positive or constructive. Positive feedback involves recognizing, rewarding, and complementing desired behaviors. Public acknowledgment of these actions encourages others to emulate them. Continuous growth and learning are essential; the day someone believes they no longer need feedback is the day they stop growing and risk becoming obsolete.

Providing Specific Feedback

When giving feedback, I focus on specific observations and how things could have been done differently. Vague statements like "good job" or "not good enough" are unhelpful. Instead, I might say, "When you asked that insightful question, it allowed us to uncover valuable information. Well done!" Conversely, in a sales call where a representative asks surface-level questions instead of probing deeper, I would suggest additional inquiries that could have yielded more information. The feedback should clearly outline what was done well and how it could have been improved.

Telling the Truth

Honesty is crucial in my approach to coaching. I strive to be as transparent as possible with my team, sharing both positive and negative results. When things are going well, we celebrate; when they're not, we address it head-on. This approach extends to my coaching style. While I acknowledge strengths, I also provide constructive criticism and identify areas for improvement. Top performers appreciate honesty and want to know where they can grow.

In one instance, I had a team member eligible for promotion, but we had limited spots for promotions. Despite her high performance and potential, others were ahead of her in terms of deserving the promotion. I informed her that she was last on the list but assured her I would advocate for her. I didn't sugarcoat the situation or make promises I couldn't keep. While the conversation was tough, she appreciated my honesty. Ultimately, I could secure her promotion, strengthening our trust and reinforcing the importance of transparency.

In another situation, I taught a team member about leading and lagging indicators and how to present them on a single-page document. After she worked diligently to create her version, I provided coaching and explained areas for improvement. However, during our video conference, I put her document through the paper shredder, which she overheard. We both laughed about it, and the incident serves as a reminder of the importance of being mindful of nonverbal cues during virtual meetings. Nonetheless, she learned the concept well and became a successful sales leader.

Areas of Improvement Versus Fatal Flaws

Areas of improvement can range from shortfalls and challenges to weaknesses that can be addressed through coaching, awareness, experience, or training. These often relate to emotional intelligence and interpersonal dynamics.

Fatal flaws, on the other hand, are behaviors that cannot be coached to improve. They are rare, but when they persist despite repeated efforts and coaching, they become indications of an unwillingness to change or an inability to recognize and address one's behaviors. While fatal flaws don't necessarily warrant dismissal from a team, they can hinder advancement opportunities. Some individuals are content with this, while others may struggle to overcome their fatal flaws.

8

Winning Hearts and Minds

Put Your Reward and Recognition Program in Writing

Documenting your reward and recognition program is critical. You get what you reward. I've seen many programs, especially as a rep, where the criteria for getting an award were unclear. Often, it seemed like the people who flattered the leadership team the most were the ones who got the awards.

One year, as a sales rep, I earned a very special award called the Eagle Award. I sat in the audience at our sales meeting, waiting for my name to be announced, but it wasn't. They had made a mistake in the criteria and didn't count a deal that would have gotten me there. At the time, it was a devastating decision and bothered me deeply. I worked hard for that recognition and was disappointed when the rules changed.

I decided that when I led my team, it would always be clear how to get an A and how team members could earn a reward. I created a reward and recognition guide. It's a physical guide that we mail to everyone at their home. I hope their spouses, partners, and significant others see it. It shows how we reward and recognize monthly, quarterly, and annual awards. It states the criteria for recognition and what you need to do to get the award.

I love rewards and recognition. It's one of the most fun parts of my job because I get to recognize incredible performances. I love talking about winners and telling personal stories about them. Leadership is very personal to me. I want people to know why they will be recognized because many say they don't like the recognition, but everybody loves to be recognized. Document your program, execute it, and make it clear and transparent to people how they can get awards on your team.

Recognize People the Way They Want To Be Recognized

I love giving people recognition for a job well done. It's an enjoyable part of my job. It builds a culture where people's efforts and results are rewarded. However, I learned a valuable lesson about tailoring recognition to an individual's preferences.

I had an exceptional HR business partner at a previous company. She significantly contributed to the organization's success, and I wanted to recognize her efforts. I created a special annual award called the Gold Key Award, which would be given to an employee who made a significant difference to the organization. I planned to present her with the award at our sales kickoff.

During the event, I took the stage and gave a heartfelt speech about the recipient's contributions to the organization. I invited her onstage, where she received a standing ovation. As I handed her the Gold Key, I noticed she wasn't smiling.

She returned to her seat, and during the first break, she asked to speak with me privately.

In our conversation, she explained that she didn't appreciate public recognition that way. She found it uncomfortable, and it didn't inspire or motivate her. I apologized and realized I hadn't considered her personal preferences when planning the recognition.

She expressed that a private conversation between us, where I sincerely expressed my gratitude for her work, would have been more meaningful to her. That's all she needed.

This experience taught me the importance of understanding how people want to be recognized. Knowing your team members' preferences is crucial to ensure your recognition efforts are valued and appreciated. Doing so can significantly enhance the impact and value of the recognition you give.

The Best Rewards and Recognition Are Personal

During my professional journey, I have been privileged to receive numerous accolades and awards. Although I appreciate each one, some stand out more vividly in my memory, not because of their grandeur but because of the deeply personal touch they carried. One such occasion remains etched in my mind.

It was during my tenure under one of the finest managers I have worked with. In a bold wager, he promised to send my wife, in-laws, mother, best friend, and me to Pebble Beach for an extraordinary event including dinner and golf, if my team achieved a specific target. The stakes were high, so I dedicated myself wholeheartedly to winning the wager. We ultimately achieved the goal and I won the bet.

As we savored an incredible dinner after our day at Pebble Beach, my father-in-law unexpectedly raised his glass for a toast. In that touching moment, he expressed his immense pride in my wife and me and acknowledged our generosity in sharing this experience with our loved ones. It was a gesture that will forever hold a special place in my heart.

This experience taught me a profound lesson. In my subsequent years as a manager, I have made it a practice to conduct what I call an "innerview." This is a conversation where I seek to understand what truly matters to each individual on my team—their priorities, aspirations, and sources of inspiration. What is their why?

One instance that vividly illustrates the impact of this approach involved a team member who shared the profound significance of her relationship with her mother. When the time came to communicate her well-deserved promotion, I took a bold step. During our video conference, I asked her to invite her mother into the room.

Tears of joy filled our eyes as I conveyed the news of her promotion in front of her mother. I took the opportunity to express my admiration for her exceptional performance and qualities as a person. It was a moment that transcended professional recognition and created an unforgettable memory for us all.

Understanding what matters most to people and tailoring their recognition has a profound impact. It transforms the act of acknowledging a job well done into a deeply personal and meaningful experience, leaving a lasting impression that resonates far beyond the immediate moment.

Small Things Make a Big Difference
Handwritten Notes: Old School Is New School

Early in my career, a leader taught me the value of writing personal notes to people. He told me that once I became a manager, I was obligated to buy custom-made, personal note cards to write notes to people. Back then, it was common for people to write notes to people, and I did it. I still have notes that leaders wrote for me back when I was a rep and a manager. I keep these notes in a file as keepsakes to remind myself that once upon a time, I knew what I was doing!

I have continued this tradition to this day. I still write thank-you notes to people; they are thoughtful, handwritten, and on my stationery. I can't tell you how many people come to me and say, "I've never had anybody at work write me a note like that. It meant so much to me. Nobody writes notes like this anymore."

People appreciate that I take the time to write these notes. For instance, at our President's Club one year, I wrote over one hundred notes to the qualifiers, each one personally written with something personal about them. I did it during the flight to the trip. I had each of them delivered to their room. This blew people away, and even more so, the spouses and guests were blown away that the executive would write a handwritten note to everyone. I understand that electronic communication has taken over the world, but I still say write a note. Old school is new school.

Look Someone in the Eye and Make Them Feel Like They Are the Only Person in the World to You at That Moment

People used to say that one of the special things about Bill Clinton was how when he talked to you, you felt like you were the only person in the world. I took that to heart and strive for that when I have one-on-one conversations with people. I look them in the eye so I don't get distracted by other people walking around, checking my email, or anything else. I try to make that person feel like they're the only person in the world. I take my notebook out and take notes, ask questions, and listen carefully. I don't always do this perfectly. It's hard to pay attention sometimes when you have so many meetings and interactions; it can be exhausting. However, I strive to make people feel like they're the only person in the world when I'm talking to them. I want them to feel special, and I want to listen and know what they're saying to me. It's an important part of leadership.

Introduce Your People with Pride

When I introduce a team member to someone, whether internally or in the marketplace, I always try to present them with pride. I will often state one of their accomplishments or something special about them and give a special introduction. I will typically stand to the side to allow the light to shine on them and give them the spotlight in front of the person I'm introducing them to.

It's part of my philosophy of always wanting people to be their best. I also want my people to know I'm proud of them. I know who they are, and they are special to me. Sometimes, I embarrass them a little by saying good things about them.

But I know deep in their hearts, they appreciate that I care about them and see them.

"I See You"

When speaking with my team members, I often tell them, "I see you." Sometimes, people wonder whether you see them and their good deeds. I go out of my way to catch people doing great things. I want them to know I know who they are and how important their contribution is to the company.

9

Creating a Winning Culture

Culture + Results = Champions

I created this equation as the core of my program. I've been on teams where everybody hated each other; we were winning, but it wasn't fun. I've also been on teams where everybody liked each other, but we weren't delivering results. Neither was any fun.

If you can build a team with a great culture and values driven by people's integrity and deliver results time after time, it will be fun while you're doing it. The place where we most exemplified that was Google X. We started the team with five people and a dog named Reggie. Reggie was a teammate's dog, a one-eyed Frenchie bulldog who would sit in our meetings, fall asleep, and snore. We all loved him and thought he would be a good mascot for our team. We determined what our values would be and practiced those values for the four years I was there, and we made sixteen quarters in a row. I greatly enjoyed being part of that team because we were true to our values and delivered great results. They go hand in hand.

Regarding the concept of culture, I've encountered various viewpoints. Some argue that culture is unimportant and self-generates, while others prioritize outcomes and relegate culture to the sidelines. In my experience, the truth lies somewhere in between. While culture does tend to develop naturally, intentional effort from leadership is crucial in shaping it. The first step involves envisioning the desired culture and seeking feedback from the team before finalizing the intended cultural values.

Culture is not merely a soft aspect but a vital factor in ensuring efficient and effective teamwork. During my time at Google X, our team of six engaged in extensive discussions to define the terms that would describe our group. Through this process, which involved arguments, disagreements, emotional moments, and laughter, we arrived at four core words: scrappy, authentic, owners, and multipliers. These words, accompanied by their associated behaviors, became the guiding principles for our team.

Remarkably, we all embraced and embodied these words, from how we conducted ourselves to how we evaluated candidates and built our culture and team. These principles remained steadfast as our company grew from a small team of five to over one hundred, and our revenue increased exponentially from $12 million to well over $200 million. They served as a unifying force during both prosperous and challenging times.

Peter Drucker's great adage, "Culture eats strategy for breakfast," holds true in my experience. A strong culture can overcome strategic inadequacies, but a weak culture can undermine even the most meticulously crafted strategy.

Create a Team Vision Board and Identity

One thing I've done with teams that has worked well is creating a team vision board. This is where my team and I workshop off-site about what we want our team's vision to be. It's not a lofty vision; it includes things we want to happen in a year, two years, or five years. We're very specific about it; sometimes, it's fun.

When I was first at Chronicle in our early days, we came up with nine things we wanted for the team over the coming years. They were kind of pie in the sky, crazy things, but it was fun to think about. I like to save things like that for the future because looking back at them is fun. I had taken this one, put it away, and hadn't looked at it for a few years. Then, one day, I picked it up and realized eight of the nine things we had dreamed about had come true. The only one that hadn't come true was that we wanted to be mentioned on Google's earnings call. It was kind of a crazy thing for a team of five to think about someday. I then put the document away again and didn't think about it.

After I left, I got a text from one of the original team members that Google's CEO had mentioned Chronicle on the earnings call. I've done this with many teams, and it's fun to see how many of the crazy, unimaginable things come true for teams when you set them up like that.

When They Don't Give You the Bad News, You're Out of Business

Leaders make a big mistake when they punish someone for delivering bad news. It discourages the team from being honest about what's happening in the field. While it's understandable to be disappointed by bad news, it's crucial to grit your teeth and encourage your team to bring it to you as quickly as possible.

I always say that the moment my team stops giving me bad news is the moment I'm on my way out of business. The reason is simple: If you don't know where the problems are in your team, you can't fix them. Problems have a way of creeping up and becoming massive issues that could put your job, or even the business, at risk.

The same applies to you when you bring up a problem. You need to foster a culture where problems are identified and addressed promptly. Flattery, sugar-coating, and avoiding the truth are sure paths to failure as a leader.

If You Ever Take Letting Someone Go Lightly, Quit Managing

Occasionally, you must let a person or a group of people go from your team. Sometimes, it's based on behavior, while others, it's solely due to business performance. Whatever the reason, if you must let someone go, you significantly impact that person's life. Whether it's their fault or not, it still substantially impacts them, potentially affecting their family and career.

Therefore, you should never take letting someone go lightly. It should bother you and trouble you. The moment you forget to feel compassion for someone who has to leave your team, you should consider leaving management. Management is a people business, and letting someone go has a lasting impact on their lives; never lose sight of that. Always take it seriously, be open, transparent, and compassionate, and allow the person to save face and retain their dignity in a challenging situation.

I have recently witnessed instances where people unfamiliar with the employee let them go, and groups were let go together on a Zoom call. I understand having one-on-one conversations with many people when you let them go is challenging. However, the moment you disregard a person's dignity and the impact it will have when asking them to leave your company, you should no longer be managing, and you should never allow any leader to put you in that situation. It usually starts at the top.

Share What You're Doing with the Families of Your Team Members

One of my most enjoyable career experiences was participating in Family Day: Bring Your Parents to X-Day. Employees of X were invited to bring their parents to visit them at X and see the interesting projects they were working on and what X looked like.

Our team took the opportunity to not only show our parents around X and the project we were working on, but we also conducted a board of directors meeting. During this meeting, the team and I presented our business, how it operated, and what we did to our parents and loved ones. It was a special moment.

I recall my uncle diligently taking notes throughout the meeting, eager to understand what we were doing. Another parent offered to refer a potential business contact to us, saying, "I have a friend who could use this." It was heartwarming to see the parents and loved ones filled with pride for their children, and it was a great opportunity for us to showcase our work.

During the pandemic, we transformed this event into something remarkable. We created a virtual "Bring Your Parents to Work" meeting. Over fifty parents and loved ones joined our team on a Zoom call, where we gave them an overview of our business, rewarded and recognized employees, and allowed our teammates to introduce their loved ones. Participants from France, Bulgaria, Middle America, and Asia came together for this call.

It was one of the most enjoyable calls I've had in my career. More importantly, it was deeply meaningful to my teammates and their families, demonstrating that they were special and valued by us. This initiative stands as a significant accomplishment during the pandemic.

The Punch List

Over time, Amy and I have completed many home improvement projects with contractors. Toward the end of a project, minor details usually need to be finished, such as repairing a piece of trim or patching a hole. These small things contribute to a polished final product. The contractors we've worked with refer to this as a "punch list," and I appreciate the term.

Whenever we have a project or a list of tasks that need to be completed as a team, I suggest creating a punch list. My team now understands that when we have a time-based project, we create a punch list. This could be a straightforward list of tasks, along with the responsible individuals and deadlines. Alternatively, it could be a series of ongoing actions and tasks that we review weekly to achieve a specific goal. I value the use of punch lists.

Communication: Tell Them Six Times in Six Different Ways

My coach, Mandy Flynt, taught me this. Early in my leadership career, I would share information about the organization via conference calls or email. When I went out into the field, people would not know what I said. Mandy taught me that if I want people to hear and remember something important, I must tell them six times in six different ways. So, when I want to communicate something important, I say it at an all-hands meeting, include it in presentations, send an email, send a video, go out into the field and communicate it directly, and so on. It's exhausting, and I get tired of saying it. However, I've found that it really sticks, and I often overhear people repeating it in the hallways.

Stop, Drop, and Roll

We had fire prevention day when I was a child and in school. A firefighter would visit us, discuss their job, and teach us survival skills in the event of a house fire. One of the most memorable lessons was the "stop, drop, and roll" technique. If you were on fire, you would stop, drop to the ground, and roll to extinguish the flames.

Recently, I found myself using the "stop, drop, and roll" analogy in a business context. When a customer has a significant issue, we should all adopt a high sense of urgency to resolve it. I like using this term with my team when encountering urgent customer-related matters. We come together, devise a plan, and collaborate with the customer to ensure the problem is resolved promptly.

There Are No Lifetime Achievement Awards

In my career, I have witnessed individuals being promoted, assigned additional responsibilities, or receiving opportunities based on their past contributions to the organization. However, within our team, I emphasize that there is no such concept as a "lifetime achievement award." Each team member must consistently demonstrate their value and dedication daily, monthly, and quarterly. High-performing teams operate this way. I do not anticipate receiving special treatment, leniency, or favoritism simply because I have been committed to the program. We must continually earn our place on the team and prove our worth daily. No one should expect free passes; we should all earn our keep. Consequently, the concept of "lifetime achievement awards" should not exist within our team.

Take a Moment To Have "A Moment" with Your Team

One thing I love to do with teams is create a moment. What does it mean to have "a moment"? These are times when something very good or challenging is happening to the team, and I want to pause the action for a minute and talk to them about what's happening.

Once, when I was with my operations leader at Google, we discussed the team's great quarter and how pleased we were with the culture and performance. She and I realized this was a special moment because we had both been on many terrible teams. Our team was relatively junior and had no idea how extraordinary this team was.

Sometimes, you don't know how good of a team you have until you leave it and experience a lousy team. So, we created something called "having a moment," where we would stop and appreciate the success of a good situation. I refer to these as "culture moments," which could be anything from a healthy conflict we learned to resolve to a series of accomplishments.

Creating these moments shows the team that you're paying attention to what's going on and trying to teach them to appreciate and recognize different moments in the business.

Sometimes, Call a Timeout to Note the Culture Moments with Your Team

Another thing I like to do is call a timeout, typically during meetings, when we're having a "culture moment." A culture moment is a special occasion you'll look back on years later as you build a championship culture. For example, a culture moment might occur when the team makes a challenging decision and achieves a positive outcome. It could also be when they have what I call a "Sicilian dinner table conversation," which is another way of saying they're having a spirited argument among themselves. Other times, it can happen when they make a difficult decision or when someone recognizes someone else for a job well done. Many moments highlight your culture. Taking a minute to recognize these moments allows the team to reflect on them, realize they're happening, and understand that these are moments we should either repeat or remember as an essential part of building a great team.

Business Is Not a Family

I often hear people say their team or company is like family. Early in my career, I said that too. However, over time, I realized that business is not like a family. In a family, you can't fire your annoying Uncle Pete. In a company, anyone can be fired and let go.

While having good relationships and caring about your coworkers is great, it's never quite like a family. Family is forever, whereas a business can end anytime, depending on the circumstances. The highest compliment I can give at work is to call a team a TEAM—in all capital letters. This means you are truly a cohesive unit. Teams can be as satisfying or even more satisfying than families, but you don't have to call it a family. It reminds me of the scene in one of my favorite movies, *The Godfather*, where Michael Corleone says, "It's business, not personal."

Performance Should Be a Natural Discussion

I try to ensure that it's crystal clear what it takes to get an A and what the minimum standards are. Then, I like to track and measure them publicly so everyone understands exactly where they stand. This applies to me as well. My performance should be highly visible.

As a result, when someone is not meeting expectations, a performance improvement plan should be a natural discussion because the expectations for performance are clear. In my experience, there are different types of performance improvement plans. There are those who are genuinely trying to coach someone who has the potential to get back on track and achieve minimum standards. Another type is where the person's behaviors will hold them back. Sometimes, someone could be achieving the performance objectives, but they're not behaving in a way consistent with the culture you're trying to build.

We employed a behavioral performance improvement plan when I was at Google. We had a top-performing rep who was great with customers but internally got into serious arguments and tried to bully someone. If they didn't change their behavior, it would hold them back. The manager had the courage to put them on a performance improvement plan for their behaviors and listed the behaviors and how they should change them. The employee took it very seriously, changed their behavior, and continued to be a top-performing manager within the team.

The third type of performance review is when someone clearly won't make the cut.

Managers should be clear at the beginning about what type of performance improvement plan they're giving to the employee.

"Who Is the Best You've Ever Worked With?"

I learned a valuable lesson from a CEO I worked for. He was one of the most skilled talent attractors I know. I watched him find such talented people. When looking for someone to fill a specific role, he would use his network and ask them, "Who is the best person you've ever worked with who did *a specific task?*"

This approach was unique and effective. By asking this question, he usually received recommendations for top candidates. I had never heard anyone ask it like that before, so I started using it myself. It changes a person's mindset when you ask them for a referral. If I simply ask, "Do you know anyone who has done this before?" I might receive a list of anyone. However, if I ask, "Who is the best you've ever worked with?" it becomes a completely different conversation. In some cases, the person may respond that they have never worked with anyone great in that particular role.

Your Personal Operating Guide

People are curious about what motivates their leaders. Trying to figure out what matters to a leader is a waste of time and energy and, frankly, creates policy. When leading a team, I prefer to share a document with them right away that I call my personal operating guide. This document outlines my leadership values, sense of purpose, and guiding principles as a leader. It also includes what makes me happy and what irritates me. Additionally, I share my personality type based on the Myers-Briggs survey.

The better my team understands who I am and how I operate, the more effectively we can work together and the more they know what to expect. By the way, avoid making your personal operating guide a personal biography. A Google executive once wrote a ten-page document about themselves. No one cares about a ten-page document about you. Keep it concise and focused so your team can easily understand who you are and what you stand for.

Avoid the "Hub and Spoke"

Leaders thrive on being in the thick of things. While I understand the sentiment, it often leads to them obstructing progress. My approach is to avoid what I term a "hub and spoke" dynamic. The "hub and spoke" analogy originates from the days of wagons, where the wheels had a central hub with spokes radiating outward, providing stability and shape to the tires.

Teams tend to operate similarly. The manager becomes the central hub through which everything must pass for completion. While well-intentioned, this structure delays processes because everyone relies on a single individual for decision-making, feedback, and task completion.

I prefer a network-based approach. I have no desire to be the linchpin of every decision. Instead, I establish a framework of goals and objectives with the team through the Victory Plan. Subsequently, I empower and encourage them to collaborate to get things done. I expect my team members to work together to achieve results without constantly seeking my involvement.

If an individual approaches me directly, treating me as the central hub, I redirect them or facilitate a meeting between relevant team members to address the issue. Over time, my team learns the importance of collaboration and self-sufficiency, reducing their reliance on me.

Off-Sites: Task Versus Relationship

Off-site gatherings can either be a productive use of time or an incredible waste. Typically, you gather a team of people at a location that incurs costs, taking them away from their usual work environment to conduct a meeting. I've participated in meetings with unclear agendas and objectives, which can be frustrating. I prefer to ensure the agenda clearly states the objectives of what we aim to accomplish.

Another crucial aspect is determining whether the meeting and agenda items will be task- or relationship-oriented. One of the common pitfalls of meetings is mixing these two types, leading to confusion about the meeting's purpose. A task-related meeting typically involves accomplishing specific tasks, such as creating a plan, reviewing the business, or conducting a talent review. These meetings have a clear goal of completing specific tasks.

On the other hand, relationship agenda items or relationship meetings focus on building teamwork through getting to know each other better, fostering trust, and establishing credibility. Examples include reviewing everyone's personal operating guide together, discussing personality types, or simply recognizing each other for their strengths and weaknesses.

It's essential to identify whether you're conducting a task-oriented or relationship meeting and communicate this clearly to the group. This clarity helps ensure everyone understands the meeting's purpose and can contribute effectively.

Go Below the Tip of the Iceberg

Problems are always deeper than they appear. As a leader, one of the most important things for me is pinpointing the problems and ensuring they are resolved. Often, when a problem is presented to me, it is only the surface level or the tip of the iceberg. This requires me to delve much deeper into the issues. I use the term "source data," which means that sometimes, as a leader, you have to go all the way down to the data source to understand where the problems lie. Until you get to the root cause of an issue, which is usually well below the high-level problem, you will not completely resolve it. This requires intellectual curiosity, attention to detail, and a desire to get to the bottom of the problem. Your best answers will come from getting as close as possible to the field at the point of contact with the customer, prospect, or partner. For instance, when I look at pipeline generated by the demand team, I often look at the logos and the dollar amounts of the opportunities. Often I find that a large total pipeline numbers can include some large deals, which indicates that many sales reps are not getting leads.

Current State Versus Desired State

One way I investigate the current state of the situation, what the desired state should be, and what barriers prevent us from reaching the desired state is by going below the iceberg. I gather this data using a combination of data, interviews, personal observations, and sometimes external data. I often use an Ishikawa diagram and a six-step solving process.

The Round Table

One of the things I tell people when joining my team is that my table is round, not rectangular. They often have a confused look on their face and ask what that means. At a rectangular table, there's always someone sitting at the head, essentially the boss. Everyone else sits at the table, reports to this person, and often looks to them to be the decision-maker.

I prefer a round table. This means we can all look each other in the eye. There is no one at the head of the table, and we all collaborate as a team. I think it's an important metaphor because it gives people an idea of what it's like to be on my team.

While I am ultimately the leader and responsible for what we do as a team, I view us all as teammates and collaborators who come up with the best ideas. I want them to know that we are all on equal footing and can contribute to the team together. I don't want to be the dictator or the sole decision-maker, so I prefer my tables round.

Teams Are Remembered; Individuals Are Forgotten

Our athletic director at St. Ignatius Prep, Leo LaRocca, once said to me, "Teams are remembered, and individuals are forgotten." I don't think I truly comprehended that statement when he said it. I thought about all the exceptional individual performers being recognized and how much our society valued individual performances. However, that statement has stayed with me for years.

As I reflect on my career now, the highest points are typically those where I'm in a photograph with others. It wasn't just about me. I've been fortunate to have many individual accomplishments, but the ones I remember most fondly are those we achieved as a team. My experience taught me, and I finally understood what he meant when he said, "Teams are remembered." When I talk about myself, I say the highest points of my career were when I worked with a group to accomplish something we thought was impossible. I now understand why Leo said, "Teams are remembered, and individuals are forgotten."

The highest compliment I can give a group of people is to call them a TEAM in all capitals. I learned this lesson from a

TriNet VP of Sales, the late Ken Williams. He taught me that a TEAM, when referred in capitals, was the highest honor you could bestow upon a group. It warms my heart to know that the companies I've been a part of still refer to themselves as a TEAM in all capitals. It takes a lot to become a TEAM.

You need collaboration, trust, and all the areas discussed in Patrick Lencioni's great book, *The Five Dysfunctions of a Team*. Most teams are what I would call either a workgroup or a loosely connected confederation of people working together. It takes hard work, commitment, and intentionality to be a TEAM.

My Off-Sites Are a Group of Chairs Arranged in a Semicircle

People are often surprised when they enter the room during my off-site meetings. I learned from a coach to set up the meeting with chairs arranged in a semicircle, flip charts, and a chair facing everyone. I do this for several reasons. First, it builds an environment of openness where no one is hiding behind a desk or table, and we are fully open to one another. It also discourages people from taking out their laptops and working during meetings. I prefer 100 percent engagement during meetings; we should be fully involved if we spend time together.

Everybody Should Have a Quantifiable Target

I create organizations where everyone has quantifiable targets that can be measured. This can be relatively easy to achieve in sales, as everyone has a quota that can be measured regularly. The Victory Plan can also assist other groups that aren't typically quantifiable. Sales engineers can have targets centered around the success of closing opportunities for technical closure. Customer success can have targets surrounding the satisfaction of their customers. Enablement can even have targets related to how sales representatives adapt to new roles and how effectively deals are closed.

One of my favorite examples of a leader being accountable was a company where the head of creative reported to me. He is the best creative leader I have ever worked with. Intrigued by how we drive accountability in the sales organization, he inquired about how to implement that in the creative organization. We collaborated to brainstorm ideas and devised a method for the creative team to measure itself through the products, projects, turnaround speed on those projects, and how those projects contributed to the company's success.

It was fascinating because he joined a best practice call with other creative leaders from highly regarded companies. No one had an answer when he asked how to create measurement and accountability within their organizations. I commend this leader because he found a way to maintain their creative excellence while striving to be accountable for the business's ultimate results.

Your Team Is a Reflection of You

When I first started as a sales representative at Gartner, our leader took great pride in his team and how we represent ourselves in the marketplace and internally within the company. He always wanted us to be our best because we reflected on him and his leadership. This created a great sense of pride in the team, and we never wanted to let our leader down. We always wanted to be the best, both internally and externally.

I have carried this philosophy with me to my teams, where I always want them to look their best in front of the market and internally. This means I coach and teach them; we practice and prepare to be our best. It truly creates a sense of pride in the team when you, as the leader, care deeply about how they present themselves. This could be anything from attention to detail in a presentation to how they speak and dress in certain situations.

It shows great care and concern for your team when you behave this way. This can also help the team, whether differentiating themselves from the competition to a prospect or how they're viewed and respected internally as a professional team. I always want sales to be the most respected team in the company because we represent what the company builds.

Sometimes, You Just Have To Force the Horse to Drink Some Water

I firmly believe in being a collaborative leader who brings people together to reach a consensus on decisions. I recognize that change can be challenging, and people need time to adapt. However, as a leader, there comes a point where you must firmly encourage people to embrace new ideas and practices.

In this regard, I use an analogy based on the old phrase, "You can lead a horse to water, but you can't make it drink." While I acknowledge that you cannot force someone to change, I sometimes believe it is necessary to nudge them in the right direction so they can experience the benefits firsthand. This approach has proven successful in my experience.

For instance, when I was at Google X, I had a few team members who were relatively inexperienced in sales. I wanted to implement changes to their compensation plan that would ultimately benefit them and the business. Understandably, people are often hesitant about changes to their compensation.

I spent considerable time explaining the rationale behind the changes and the potential benefits for everyone involved. Despite my efforts, I eventually had to firmly push them to accept the new plan.

Fortunately, at the end of the year, both team members were incredibly pleased with the revised compensation plan. It worked as anticipated, and they expressed their gratitude for the changes.

If I had not provided that final nudge, they might not have embraced the new plan, which could have had negative consequences for the business and their personal growth.

Leadership Is Lonely; You Are the Decider

I recall a dark winter evening in an office as I faced a challenging decision. No one else was present—just me. I had gathered all available data, information, opinions, and feedback, and the decision rested upon my shoulders. I knew this choice would greatly impact my team and potentially jeopardize my career. The concept of leadership being a lonely endeavor came to mind.

Ultimately, as a leader, it is my responsibility to make decisions. Despite gathering input, reviewing data, and listening to team members' perspectives, the final choice lies with me.

This burden of decision-making can be isolating, particularly when faced with potential failure.

I have faced moments of solitary decision-making in my office, which I call the War Room. Often, at the end of the day, in the dimly lit room, the responsibility to make tough choices falls solely upon me. The outcome, success or failure, rests entirely on my shoulders.

Two great leaders I admire are George Washington and Dwight Eisenhower. In Valley Forge, Washington sought solitude and prayed for success. His decision would determine the war's outcome, and I imagine the profound loneliness he must have felt. Similarly, Eisenhower had to make the pivotal decision of when to launch D-Day. Amidst unpredictable weather and a narrow window of opportunity, he sat with his generals and bore the burden of a decision that would affect tens of thousands of lives.

Before the invasion, he visited the troops at the front line, finding solace in their unwavering belief in him and the cause. He even drafted a press release assuming full responsibility in case of failure.

These examples highlight leadership's inherent loneliness. Ultimately, the decision-making responsibility lies with the leader alone, and no one else bears the consequences.

People Get On and Off the Bus

People often get upset and stressed when someone leaves the team. Additionally, they get stressed when a new person joins the team and how it impacts change. When talking to my team, I like to use the bus analogy. In this analogy, the bus driver is typically the CEO or another C-level executive. The bus is headed in a specific direction, and it's up to the leader to drive it in that direction. The leader is also responsible for ensuring everyone is in the right seat on the bus to reach the desired destination.

At times, someone may decide that it's time for them to get off the bus. This could be because they don't want to continue to the destination, they've had a great ride and want to move on, or they're unable to go to the next destination. It's okay to get off the bus.

At the same time, there will be people who get on the bus and sit in a certain spot, and they will be the ones to continue the next part of the journey. It's okay to get on and off the bus. It's a natural part of business.

Expectations for a Vice President

I like to ensure my direct reports, typically a vice president, understand my expectations for their role. An operations leader I worked with told me a story about Steve Jobs. (I don't know if it's true. There are many stories about the legendary Steve Jobs that may or may not have happened.)

Anyway, this story was about Steve Jobs explaining his expectations for executives. If a janitor is expected to clean an office and the door is closed, the janitor will check the door, and if it doesn't open, they will move on to the next office. Steve Jobs' expectation for a vice president executive would be that they can't merely walk away if they need to clean an office or get something done because the door won't open. They must be creative and find a way. This could involve anything from going through the window on the other side of the room to kicking the door down or vaporizing themselves—whatever they need to do to get into that office and clean it. This was an expectation Steve Jobs had for his executives.

I have a similar expectation for my leaders. When we need to get something done, we do whatever we can think creatively to find a way to get the job done. We can't just move to the next office. One of my leaders used to say, "I am going to go vaporize to get that task done." I loved that.

Win like You Expected It

I love watching coaches and observing their behavior in various situations. One of my role models and favorite coaches is Coach K. There's a video I enjoy showing my team at the end of a quarter at the year's end. It showcases a series of last-second buzzer beaters by the Duke Blue Devils, coached by Coach K. It's truly inspiring to witness all the team's buzzer beaters.

What I find most intriguing about that video is that almost every time a Duke player makes one of those buzzer beaters, you see Coach K stand up and walk toward the opponent's bench to shake their hands. He doesn't jump around or run all over the place; he behaves as if he expected his team to do this. It really inspires me to think about how we behave as leaders. As Coach Wooden would say, "The highs can't be too high, and the lows can't be too low." We must expect our teams to be successful and show them that we expect them to be successful.

Another thing I've noticed about Coach K and Steve Kerr is that when their teams win the championship and the celebration begins and the awards are given out, they both stand to the side and let their teams and players receive all the rewards and accolades. They don't want to be in the spotlight; they want their teams to be in the spotlight. I love that. I believe it's true leadership to want your people to be successful and let them take the glory. Give your team all the credit when things go well; when things go wrong, we should take all the responsibility as leaders.

Sometimes, Give Feedback Using Pictures

Once, I was thinking about how to provide coaching and feedback to one of my direct reports. This person was very visual and preferred simple, clear guidance on improving their sales performance. After giving it considerable thought, I identified the three or four key areas where they needed to improve to become the successful executives they aspired to be. I decided to use images to convey my feedback.

For instance, this person tended to get upset quickly in certain situations because they were very protective of their organization. To address this, I found a picture of Yoda and used it to illustrate that impulsively reacting wasn't in their best interest. I explained that, like Yoda, it was better to stay calm, take time, and think through the situation before reacting. I provided similar visual feedback in other areas.

They loved it. They took a copy of the images and hung it above their desk in their home office as a reminder to reflect on their daily behavior.

Create a Team of Crazies

When I first joined X, our project team consisted of people with different skills, and we all did everything. As a team leader, I even handled support cases—probably not very well—but it demonstrated that we all shared the workload. As we grew, hired more people, and added more managers, a group of three or four people from the early days had skills that didn't quite fit into a standard role. So, I created a small team called "the crazies."

These were the people who always thought outside the box, constantly coming up with creative ideas, finding ways to automate processes, and doing things differently. They didn't fit into a typical job description or role, but they were exceptional at accomplishing what seemed impossible. I loved that team because they understood our mission and objectives, were smart and creative, and always found ways to get things done—sometimes in unorthodox ways. It taught me that having a small, dedicated team focused on creative solutions is a great asset to any business.

The team even created stickers with my picture and a funny design that said, "I want crazies." We were trying to get our product on an internal marketplace. It was challenging because there were limited resources, and the marketplace was relatively new. We knew it could be one of the most important drivers of our business, but the odds of getting on the marketplace seemed low. So, we turned our "crazy" team loose on the problem. They built internal relationships, identified helpful people in different departments, and modified our product to make it easier to get on the marketplace. Against the odds, we succeeded in getting our product on the marketplace.

This was just one example of what a creative, fun team can accomplish, and looking back, it was part of the secret sauce that made our team successful.

Tales from the Road

Manny Fernandez, the CEO of Gartner, was beloved by the salesforce. He was always willing to roll up his sleeves and get out in the field with salespeople to create and close business. Every year at the sales kickoff, he would do something called "Tales from the Road." He would share three or four of the best stories from his time in the field, tell the story, and then give the person involved a humorous token as a reminder of that experience. I was once recognized with this award for a meeting I arranged with him and a CEO he disliked. He gave me a hard hat, which I treasure to this day.

This inspired me to create my own "Tales from the Road" while leading my organization. Since I spent much of my time in the field with prospects, customers, and partners, I began recording short thirty-second videos on my phone with different people I met. I would then share these videos with the organization. It quickly became popular, and people started inviting me into the field to be part of the tales. On one occasion, I even asked a prospect to share a video of his thoughts about TriNet and why he might become a customer. He enjoyed it, and ultimately, he did become a customer.

This approach was a great way to connect with the field, see what was happening on the ground, and let others share those experiences.

Understanding and Leading the Change Curve

Naturally, people hate change. They say they like change, but nobody likes change. One of the things I've learned over time is the change curve. This is the period people accept change. They typically go through awareness, excitement, disappointment, and then acceptance.

My job as the team leader is to always be ahead of the team—to be well ahead of the team in the change curve with a vision of where we want to go. It's my job to walk the team through each stage of the change curve. As leaders, we must also consider the people on our team who the change will impact.

One time, when I took over a team, one of my direct reports didn't seem like he was accepting the change and seemed resistant to me as the new leader. He had been very dedicated to the previous leader and saw him as a mentor. Because I thought he was not getting on board, I had a one-on-one with him two weeks after I took over and challenged him on why he was not getting with the program. It was a big mistake. I did not realize this person was going through the change curve. Fortunately, I got some good coaching and could coach myself and this person to agree to the change curve. I gave him more room and time to process. I asked him how he was feeling and what he was thinking about the change. I listened to him and what was important to him. I also shared what I thought the future would look like and the opportunities he would have. Building relationships takes time. Luckily, we both got coaching before I lost this person. He was probably one of the best people I've ever worked with. I would put him on my top-ten list of all the managers who have ever reported to me.

Teaching your leadership team about the change curve, understanding it, and leading your team through the change curve is critical. Too often, leaders stand up and say we're making this change today, and everybody must get on board. That is a big mistake. Understand that people don't like change; they take time to adapt to it, and it's up to us as leaders to lead them through change.

Shoelaces, the Heart, the Fist, No Scoreboards

I love using pictures and analogies to get a point across. I'm a natural storyteller, and people love pictures because they appeal not only to their auditory learning but also visually.

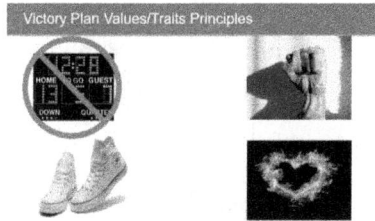

Victory Plan Values/Traits Principles

I like using visuals to make a point

Over time, I've learned there are four keys to building a championship sales team.

1. **Shoelaces:** When John Wooden was the coach of the UCLA Bruins, one of the most successful college basketball teams of all time, he would spend one entire practice showing his team how to put their socks on and tie their shoelaces. He attended to every detail because he thought attending to every detail would help the team win. Why shoelaces? Because if your socks are not put on correctly, you could get blisters. If your shoes aren't tied, they could become untied during a game and put your team at a disadvantage. This type of attention to detail enabled the UCLA Bruins to be a winning program. I do the same thing with my teams. When somebody misses a detail, we use the term shoelaces, which reminds us to attend to the smallest details to ensure the team is successful.

2. **The heart:** I learned this from Coach K. People have hearts, dreams, and desires. Everyone has a different desire and motivation. Our job as leaders is to understand what is in each person's heart and create a situation and environment for a team that appeals to what's most important to their hearts. People are not robots. They never will be; they will always have hearts. It's our job as leaders to appeal to their hearts. I think old-school leadership treated people like robots. Coach K, Mike Krzyzewski, and the Duke Blue Devils men's basketball team leadership style resonated with me. It was driven by treating people like individuals and leading them with heart. Coach K leads with heart and passion. He gets to know what's important to all his players, why they do what they do, and appeals to their hearts, not just their minds. It's a different leadership style that was less popular forty years ago when I started. However, it's become very popular over time.

3. **The fist:** This is another one I learned from Coach K. Trying to punch somebody with your hand open and fingers apart is unsuccessful. Just try it, but don't break your finger. When you put all five of those fingers together into a fist, you can punch your fist through a wall. Teams are the same way. If everybody acts like an individual or a workgroup, you easily get divided and don't fight in the market successfully. If everybody comes together as one, like a fist, you win. Same goes for sales. Everybody must play as a team, even though there are individual performer characteristics.

4. **No scoreboards:** I've learned this from several coaches, including Bill Walsh. I always got tight, nervous, and worried whenever I looked at the business results

before the end of the quarter or year. The point is to focus on your process and your program. If you execute your program and process flawlessly, the scoreboard will take care of itself. I've learned not to stare at the result but to look at the process.

Every Time You Add a New Team Member, You Start Over

Building a team is hard work and takes intentionality. Many leaders want to just move forward and tell everybody to get on with it. That's not how I operate. Everybody has to understand the plan, the program, who we are, each other's strengths and weaknesses, and how we operate as a team.

When you bring a new team member on, you have to introduce that new member to your program. Everybody has to get to know who that person is and what makes them tick. The new person needs to understand what makes the individuals in the group tick. It's hard work because you have to stop the bus, let everybody get off, understand where we're going, get back on, and start again.

You won't be as successful if you don't slow down to allow a new member to get acclimated to the team. New members change the dynamics of a team. Therefore, you must always take time to understand the dynamics and how the team will work together.

When I was appointed the VP of the Technology Sales Organization at Symantec, I used to refer to myself as "the double devil." I was not a deep technologist. I was not from Europe but was asked to lead a very important team there. Before I took the role, a book called *Team of Rivals* came out. It was a story of how, when Abraham Lincoln became president, he asked several of his rivals who he had defeated in the election to join his cabinet. It could be one of the best leadership books I've ever read because instead of vanquishing his rivals, Lincoln reached out to them and asked for their assistance for the union's good. It was a magnanimous decision and one that was very risky. Seward, Stanton, and others served as cabinet members to Lincoln and significantly contributed to the government's success and the ultimate victory in the Civil War. These former rivals were devastated by Lincoln's death. One of them was quoted as saying that Lincoln was the greatest leader he had ever known.

It was a similar situation when I came to Europe. Everyone who reported to me had applied and interviewed for the job. I had to decide whether I wanted to be confrontational or welcoming to all. I was fortunate to have an amazing HR business partner who worked alongside me as we reached out and built relationships with all those leaders. I sat with each of them and understood what their priorities were. I incorporated them into how we built the Victory Plan together. They were integral in how we built the culture.

By the end of the three-year assignment, every leader on the team improved. One of the original leaders had developed into someone who could take over the next generation, and I conducted a presidential handoff. This is where we had a formal transition from me to the team's next leader. We did it ceremonially before the team. At the end, we shook hands. I walked away and left my previous office, moving into a small office off to the side. He took over my office and became the next leader. These are all lessons I learned from Lincoln.

They Who Have the Hardline Rules the Day

I have worked in many matrix organizations throughout my career. This is where an individual reports directly to one manager and has a dotted line report to another. While this can be a very effective organizational structure, it can become confusing and a waste of resources if not well understood.

In my experience, whoever holds the direct (hardline) reporting relationship has the most influence over the individual. If you can hire, fire, or provide performance feedback that impacts someone's job, there will naturally be a stronger connection. This isn't necessarily a bad thing, but it's important to understand that if you're the dotted line manager, the person will, under pressure, typically defer to the hardline manager.

The best way to manage this dynamic is to ensure you have a strong relationship with the other manager and that your metrics are aligned. In my experience, nine times out of ten, conflicts between managers from different parts of the organization arise because their goals are not aligned. Companies encounter this issue frequently; alignment is key to avoiding such conflicts.

Thirty Seconds of Fame

I remember a meeting led by John Besteman, one of the best leaders I've ever worked for. It was a team meeting with about thirty people, and we had worked together for two days. At the end of the second day, he did something called "Thirty Seconds of Fame." He allowed each person to say something at the end of the meeting; it could be anything they wanted. They could share their thoughts about the meeting, mention something they were thinking about, or even talk about their love for the Boston Red Sox, as one person did.

It was an incredible way to close the meeting because, invariably, everyone had something positive to say, and it built wonderful momentum. It also allowed everyone to speak their mind and share their thoughts before leaving. I've carried this practice into all my meetings since, and I've found it to be incredibly effective. Yes, sometimes people express frustration at the end of a meeting, but in my experience, 99 percent of the time, they express gratitude and appreciation for the meeting, people, and outcomes. I love "Thirty Seconds of Fame."

What I Learned by Creating a Women's Leadership Group

When I started at TriNet, there were very few women leaders in the Sales organization. One of my core values is finding the gold in all people and seeking talent wherever it can be found. So, with my HR business partner, we decided to create a women's leadership group. We wanted to develop the next generation of women in the organization because we had many great, high-potential individuals.

At one of our sales kickoffs, we launched this initiative, gathering thirty high-potential women in a room. The power in that room nearly knocked me over. The amount of energy, passion, and intelligence was incredible. In fact, after a while, they told me I could leave because they were ready to take it from there. Many of those women became future leaders in the organization, helping TriNet become one of the top-fifty selling organizations in American business. I was incredibly proud of what they achieved. I'll never forget the power and energy in that room during our first meeting.

Beware of the Empire Builder

Every organization has leaders who derive their sense of purpose from the size of their organization and the number of people or functional areas that report to them. For these "empire builders," personal power is their purpose. This is often driven by poor self-esteem or a need to feel important. As Peter Drucker says, "The purpose of an executive is to deliver results." The fatal flaw of the empire builder is that they judge their importance by the number of people who report to them, not by the contribution they make.

Drucker writes in what is likely the best book ever written, The Effective Executive, about being an executive, "The man who focuses on efforts and who stresses his downward authority is a subordinate no matter how exalted his title and rank. But the man who focuses on contribution and who takes responsibility for results, no matter how junior, is in the most literal sense of the phrase, 'top management.' He holds himself accountable for the performance of the whole."

The number of people or organizations you lead is not an indicator of your effectiveness. An executive must always think about what contribution the company needs and what they can deliver to advance its goals. Executives who focus on their organization's size often miss this critical point. Most of the time, the empire builder disrupts the organization's ability to deliver results. Politics becomes a priority over influencing outcomes for the organization's greater good, leading to wasted time on internal issues instead of advancing the company.

Effective executives who know how to focus on results rather than effort often confront the empire builder head-on, which distracts them from what is most important: delivering results.

This is a fatal mistake because the executive ends up fighting at the subordinate level of the empire builder rather than operating as "top management."

High Potential Development Programs Drive Higher Productivity

Short-sighted leaders don't invest in their people. They claim it's a waste of time and money and need immediate results. We received this kind of feedback when we created a high-development program at TriNet. "Why are we taking them out of the field? Why are we wasting their time? We're going to lose productivity. How are we going to make our quota?" These were all questions some asked when I launched the program.

We worked with Jay Tyler from JTC and launched the Braveheart Program. We tracked participants' performance through the program. We had twenty people in that first class and tracked the number of meetings, proposals, pipeline, and closed deals for that group. Yes, they had to spend time outside of their day-to-day work on projects, classroom time, and working on their individual Victory Plans. It was a game changer. At the end of the program, their productivity had increased by over 30 percent compared to when they started. They became more productive.

Why? First, we developed them and gave them new techniques to become better businesspeople. Second, they felt special, incredibly motivated, and inspired by the investment we were making in them as professionals and as people. This increased their dedication and commitment to the company. I would make that decision a hundred times. It was a great investment, and we positively impacted these people's lives.

10

Leading Yourself... And Your Boss

Do Your Best To Be Your Best

There are so many lessons to take from Coach John Wooden, whose UCLA Bruins have won more NCAA Basketball Championships than any other team in history. His team's records will probably never be broken for the number of NCAA Basketball Championship wins.

The one lesson that has stuck with me most over the years is that he would tell his team, "Always do your best to be your best." It was never about defeating the opposition but always about being your best. He believed that if you did your best to be your best, regardless of winning or losing, you would be successful. Not focusing on the outcome but focusing on myself and my team being the best at running our program has carried me through in leadership. Also, I never say I give 110 percent. You can only give 100 percent of your effort.

"Success is peace of mind, which is a direct result of self-satisfaction in knowing you did your best to become the best you are capable of becoming."
—John Wooden

The Highs Cannot Be too High, and the Lows Cannot Be too Low

As an authentic sales leader, you'll be close to the action and often quickly receive good or bad news. The key for a sales leader is not to let emotions get the best of you; don't get too excited when something good happens or too disappointed when something bad happens. Your team relies on you to demonstrate stability.

Laser Focus: Make Sure Your Task Is Crystal Clear

I've observed when joining new teams that the sales team's goals are often not clearly defined. You would think this would be a basic requirement for any team. I remember joining one company where three different numbers were used interchangeably: the board's number, an aspirational company number, and the chief revenue officer's number.

I ensure the task is completely clear and agreed upon from the start. What is the one number we're all going to publicly commit to? This doesn't mean you can't have a different number for the board or an aspirational target, but when communicating with the field and the team, there should only be one number that everyone is striving for. This clarity of purpose creates focus and energy within the team.

Get Some Great Coaches

When I think of some of the greatest athletes of all time, like Michael Jordan, Lebron James, and Kobe Bryant, they all had coaches. Some of them had multiple coaches for how to eat the right diet, stretching and flexibility, psychology, massage and recovery, and all kinds of people who helped the greatest be the greatest. Why would the greatest athletes need these coaches? Because they always wanted the edge. They were hungry to get better. They knew they had their limits and wanted to find ways of taking themselves to the next level through coaching.

Businesspeople are the same way. I was fortunate to have two coaches who greatly impacted my career: Mandy Flynt and Isabella Conti. Mandy was my coach when I moved to Europe. I was probably on the edge of failure because I was leading a five-hundred-person team in the same way I was leading a fifty-person team. I was not succeeding and was unaware of my behaviors and how the rest of the team was taking them. I was lucky enough to receive a coach who performs personality assessments and a 360 about me and my leadership. The feedback was incredible. We did a day-long session to review all the feedback. I went to bed at 6:30 that night because I was so exhausted. We created a coaching plan that made all the difference in the world. I have no doubt that coaching greatly contributed to my success.

Isabella was my coach at TriNet when I joined the CEO's table for the first time. There were many things I didn't know about how to be at a CEO's table, but Isabella took the time to understand who I was, what was important to me, and the feedback from the leadership team about me. We worked on that feedback, which contributed to my success as an executive at TriNet and a future leader at the CEO's table.

How We Think Controls How We Feel

Victor Frankl wrote one of the most impactful books I've ever read, *Man's Search for Meaning*. I read it every year. The first part is his account of his experience at the Auschwitz Nazi concentration camp. In the second half, he discusses his philosophies and psychological approach based on what he learned. I gain new insights from this book every time I read it, but the most important one is that no one could take away his thoughts when he was in the concentration camp. They could take his physical dignity and break him physically, but they could never control how he thought about things. I was fortunate to read this book as a young person, and it taught me that we can control how we think and respond to situations.

As authentic sales leaders, we can determine whether something is good or bad and how we respond to it. We always have the option to respond to things positively, even in the face of adversity. Our team relies on our positive attitude to keep their spirits up.

No Surprises!

I recall someone giving a lecture or talk and asking how many audience members enjoyed surprises. Most people raised their hands. However, the speaker then said, "No, you only like good surprises!"

Reflecting on that, I realized as a leader, I don't appreciate surprises. I prefer to be predictable and follow through on my commitments. While I may appreciate a surprise deal or unexpected opportunity, I tend to respond with a slap on the wrist and a warning not to repeat such behavior. Delivering bad news without warning will elicit a negative reaction from me.

One thing that particularly irks me is when someone surprises me with a drop in their forecast in front of a group of people. It's acceptable to inform me privately and separately about any issues. Timely communication of bad news is appreciated, but surprises are generally not well-received.

Similarly, I never like to surprise my boss—even with good news.

Don't Miss One-on-Ones with Your Boss

Sometimes, when you are doing a great job, your boss will say you can skip your one-on-one. I don't like skipping one-on-ones because I like a constant communication link to my manager. I don't need them to hold my hand all day or ask what I'm doing every day. However, I like a regular line of communication to ensure they're always aware and never surprised about what's happening. This is why I use the template and am always as transparent as possible with my manager. I never want them to be surprised.

Therefore, if they say they will miss the one-on-one, ask to reschedule to a fifteen-minute talk and make sure you have that connection. You don't have to be (and shouldn't be) best friends with your boss, but you should have an open line of communication and keep the discipline of having regular one-on-one meetings with your manager.

Maniacal Execution: The One-Hundred-Day Plan

I remember when I was first a rep at Gartner and noticed how the head of sales always had a big initiative for the year that he would launch at the sales kickoff. It seemed odd to me because, typically, the leader would never talk about what they had done in the previous year or the successes and failures of the program from the previous year. Then, I had the privilege of working for a mentor, Jim Dougherty, who taught me to always share with the team what I had done in the past before I did something new. He taught me to prioritize what I did and be very clear about my priorities.

I have learned this over time: Executives can barely execute one thing—let alone fifty things. Most people I work with, particularly those early in their careers, tend to work on multiple priorities because they think they're getting a lot done. I've learned that choosing three to five key priorities and actions associated with them is an effective way to get things done.

So, I like to create a one-hundred-day plan where I identify three to five things that I will absolutely make sure I execute. I work with my boss, and we rate our priorities. We also determine how much time I will spend on them. Then, we shake hands and agree I'll execute them.

During my regular one-on-one updates with my boss, I update them on how I'm doing with those priorities. I also share these priorities with my direct reports, team, and peers so everybody knows what I will execute. It's a risky strategy because it's very public if you don't execute something. However, I'm not the type of leader who likes to hide what I have or haven't done. Be transparent and courageous when executing. It demonstrates the behavior you want in your team.

Often, when I coach individuals, it is because their inexperienced CEO fails to grasp the importance of prioritizing their time. Regardless of one's role, prioritizing time allocation is essential. It is disheartening to work diligently on a task only to have one's boss later criticize the omission of other tasks. It is imperative to clarify expectations, document agreements, and diligently execute the plan to avoid this.

Organize Your Thoughts with a Mind Map

When I was in Europe with Symantec, I noticed people drawing pictures with numerous circles and lines on them. It was unfamiliar to me, and everyone seemed to be using them. I inquired about these diagrams, and someone introduced me to mind maps.

A mind map is essentially a visual representation of a core topic with related issues. It's a brainstorming methodology that results in a picture showing the core topic, related issues, and further related issues.

Mind maps are an effective way to organize thoughts and ideas into a single-page document. While there are technologies for mind mapping, I find that a traditional piece of paper and a pen work best.

A JT Mindmap

I use mind maps to plan priorities for the coming year, prepare for significant presentations, and create narratives for board meetings. My team is now familiar with this approach, as I often create mind maps during quiet, uninterrupted times, such as long plane flights. I then photograph and send them to my team, who can easily see my progress.

They then say, "It looks like JT's been working on mind maps again." Mind maps help me organize my thoughts.

There Is Always Someone in the Back of the Room Waiting to Kick You

I credit Harvey McKay for this insightful advice. Initially, as a first-time manager with a small team, I didn't fully grasp its significance. However, experience has taught me that assuming everyone is on board with your plans can be a costly mistake. In sales, for instance, you may encounter a prospect who appears agreeable, but there might be someone quietly lurking in the background, waiting for the right moment to undermine your efforts. This individual, often called a saboteur, can also exist within your company. Those who agree with you will typically express their support, and you might see a roomful of nodding heads. However, someone is often in the corner, biding their time, waiting for you to make a mistake, say the wrong thing, or expose you. Recognizing this reality has prevented me from assuming I have a complete consensus and that everyone is fully committed to our goals. Instead, I am always considering contingencies and thinking about the future. It's almost inevitable that someone, out of the blue, will create a roadblock, challenge, or attack you. Be prepared for this eventuality.

Plan B Sucks

At a sales kickoff, the keynote speaker was Chris Gardner, the author of the book *The Pursuit of Happyness*, which later became a movie. It is one of my favorite films. During his keynote, he said, "Plan B sucks." That stuck with me. His point was that successful people, such as Michael Jordan,

Oprah Winfrey, and Barack Obama, were all successful because they were 100 percent committed to their plan. There was no Plan B, which is the point. You have to be 100 percent committed to your goals. As Chris says, "If Plan B were good, it would be Plan A."

Chris Gardner taught us that "Plan B Sucks"

Nothing Good Happens After 10PM

I was fortunate to learn this from an executive early in my career. I noticed that at big meetings, around 9:00 p.m., he would order a glass of chardonnay at the bar, take it with him, and head up to his room. Everyone else, including other executives, would stay out, drinking and having a great time. Later, I asked him why he went to his room with his glass of chardonnay. He said, "JT, nothing good ever happens after 9:00 p.m. As a manager, people will approach you. Your power may attract them, and alcohol may lower your inhibitions; you could end up doing something stupid. So, I take my glass of wine, go up to my room, get a book, read for a while, and then go to bed."

It was an invaluable lesson. During that time, I saw some executives make poor decisions—one passed out at the bar and had to be escorted back to his room, while another invited an employee to their room, which ultimately impacted their marriage.

When I became a manager, I practiced the same discipline. At big meetings and dinners, I always made it a point to head back to my room by 9:00 p.m. I never went to the hotel bar, never visited nightclubs, and always made sure I was in control. While I don't drink alcohol, I would go up to my room, relax, read, and get ready for bed. I never regretted that decision.

Mad Decisions Lead to Bad Decisions

Whenever I make a decision out of anger or frustration, there's a 90 percent chance it will be bad. This is because I'm usually reacting to something someone has told me or a situation I've seen. It's always better to take a step back, take a deep breath, and think about the decision. I've often found that sleeping on an angry decision changes my mind the next morning.

The same goes for how I react to people and situations that frustrate me. My first reaction is usually not my best one. It doesn't mean that my gut feeling is wrong; it just means that my immediate response won't always be the best one. I've learned that the bigger the team you lead, the more important it is to avoid making emotional decisions. They often have implications you haven't thought through and will be bad decisions.

Taking a step back, looking at the data, and speaking with people you trust before making a decision, even if you're angry or frustrated, is a much better policy and will lead to better decisions.

It's Time To Go when Your Company's Values Don't Align with Yours

There will be times when you're in a company, and the company's values start to change. Sometimes, this is a natural evolution of a company, while other times, it's due to new leadership.

I once joined a company that brought in a new executive leadership team. They were all talented individuals, but as I met with several of them, I noticed they would speak poorly about each other. The CEO exhibited questionable personal behaviors.

After a manager's meeting, I witnessed one of these executives engage in inappropriate behavior in front of two of my high-potential leaders who were sitting with me. We left soon after, and while in the taxi heading back to our hotel, both looked at me and asked, "Is this where the company is going?"

I was embarrassed by the question because I agreed with them. Soon after, I spoke with that same executive who commented to me about his values aligning with mine. However, I thought they didn't align, as I didn't believe in behaving that way or think it was a good example for our employees.

This incident created doubt in my mind about the company's future. I decided it was time to leave because the values the management and leadership teams demonstrated did not align with mine.

I eventually left the company. That team was ultimately unsuccessful and replaced by another management team. While this may not always be the case, I felt good about my decision because I didn't want to be part of an organization's leadership team that didn't align with my values.

How To Pick Your Next Job

One morning, I was having breakfast with Kelly Kay, senior partner at Heidrick and Struggles, one of the world's most respected recruiting firms. I had the privilege of being placed by him, and we were discussing how to decide on the next step in one's career. While eating our bacon and eggs, he rattled off a process for considering one's next role. I asked him to slow down, and I wrote down what he said. I've since used this process to consider all my next roles.

First, I brainstorm all the things that are important to me about work and any personal aspects of my life that relate to work. I usually end up with a few pages of things that are important to me. Then, I remove duplicates, categorize them, and prioritize the categories based on their importance to me.

From this exercise, I typically have three to five things that are important to me about what I want to do next. This can change over time. My current job will often match all these important things, so there's no reason to consider leaving. Sometimes, they won't match, and I'll start thinking about my next opportunity.

This process clarifies what's next for me and, more importantly, provides recruiters and hiring managers clarity on what I want to do next. Most recruiters and hiring managers try to match the person to the job. The clearer you can be about what you want and what's important to you, combined with your background, skills, and capabilities, the higher the probability you'll find a role you'll love and one that matches what's important to you.

Go Back and Review Your Big Decisions

About every six months, I like to go back and review major decisions I have made. These could be personal or work-related decisions. I enjoy revisiting my notes to reflect on my thought process at the time, considering the pros and cons, and assessing the information available to me. I then evaluate the implications of those decisions. Were they beneficial? How might I have approached them differently? Most people I know make significant decisions and then move on without looking back. In my opinion, this is a missed opportunity to improve your decision-making skills. Ultimately, as a leader, your responsibility is to make decisions. Learning from positive and negative experiences and incorporating those lessons into future choices will contribute to your growth as a leader.

You Never Know

I have heard this said many times, but I have rarely seen it practiced. I remember someone once telling me common sense is not common practice. I see this all the time in how people treat others. Managers often look down on others because they think they are better than them.

When I was an officer at First Interstate Bank early in my career, someone taught me that you should always treat everyone like they are the most important customer in the bank. One Friday afternoon, a man walked in. He was shabbily dressed, quite disheveled, and asked, "Can somebody help me?" I walked up and treated this man as if he were the most important customer. We sat down, and he had a FedEx envelope from which he took out a check worth millions of dollars. He said he had just sold one of his hotels in San Francisco. He apologized for looking so disheveled, explaining that he had been painting his house and wanted to deposit the check. He opened an account and became one of the bank's best customers.

Another example of treating everyone with dignity and respect comes from my time at Symantec. A junior finance person had just started working with our team. Most other sales leaders were not very kind to him, but I took the time to get to know him and help him adjust to his new role. We both moved on after a while, and I didn't think much more about it. However, when I was interviewing at TriNet, the CEO liked to do back-channel references on candidates. He called someone I didn't know he would call to find out what I was like to work with. It just so happened that the junior finance person from my Symantec days was the CEO's favorite nephew. The CEO asked him what it was like to work with me, and he was very complimentary, saying that I was the only person who demonstrated kindness to him when he was in that role. I am grateful I treated him with respect because if he had given me a negative reference, I likely wouldn't have gotten the job. Interestingly, that person became one of the best operations leaders I have ever worked with. I am fortunate to have had the opportunity to work with him.

Treat everyone with dignity and respect, no matter who they are or who you think they are. It's simply the right thing to do.

Old Grizzlies and How To Be a Great Mentee

I recall reading about finding an "old grizzly" (men and women!) early in my career. An old grizzly is someone who has experienced numerous battles, bearing the scars and scrapes of their mistakes and struggles. These individuals possess valuable knowledge and wisdom they can share with others.

I was fortunate enough to find a few old grizzlies who became mentors to me. They had already made the mistakes I was likely to make and could caution me against foolish decisions. Old grizzlies are often difficult to find because they don't typically flaunt their scars and battles to everyone. You have to go out of your way to seek them out. However, when you find one, hold on to them tightly because their knowledge is invaluable.

The old grizzlies I've worked with have been a source of immense gratitude to me. They helped me avoid many mistakes and make the best decisions of my career. They appreciated my eagerness to learn and my genuine curiosity about their thoughts and ideas. I took their advice, applied it, and always reported back to them with the results.

One of the most important aspects of being a great mentee is taking your mentor's advice and reporting the results. One of the most influential mentors in my career was my next-door neighbor, Dick Boucher, a retired Intel executive who had led global HR and legal departments. He was a humble man who always made time to meet with me and offer guidance. Whenever I brought him work challenges, he listened attentively and gave thoughtful advice. He would jot down notes on a yellow legal pad, making me feel like my problems mattered. I made it a point to return to him later and share the outcomes of his feedback and recommendations. Sometimes, they worked. Sometimes, they didn't, but he derived great joy from knowing he could help someone early in their career. I would not have succeeded without his mentorship.

Nothing satisfies an old grizzly more than knowing you tried their suggestion, even if it didn't work. If it does work, it warms their heart. If it doesn't, they appreciate that you at least gave it a shot and reported back to them. Many people have sought my advice over the years, but I have no idea if they acted on it because they never came back to me with the results. This lack of feedback is unsatisfying.

Read History and Biography—Not Business Books (Unless it's mine)

Early in my career, I read all the business books. One of my mentors looked at all the business books I was reading and asked why I didn't read history and biography, saying that's where I'd learn the best business lessons. So, I started reading more biographies and fiction. I learned many leadership lessons from books like *Master of the Senate* by Robert Caro (about Lyndon Johnson) and *Playing the Enemy* about Nelson Mandela. World War II books about the invasion of Normandy, General Eisenhower, and Julius Caesar taught me even more business and leadership lessons than I could have ever learned by reading today's business books. There are only ten to fifteen business books that I think were truly valuable and have stood the test of time.

There Is no Such Thing as a Confidential Conversation

There's absolutely no such thing as a confidential conversation; don't let anyone fool you. Why do I say this? When you share confidential information with someone and tell them it's confidential, no matter how much you think you trust them, there's a natural inclination for them to use that information as currency. We all love having information that others don't; it feels empowering to say to someone, "Hey, this is confidential. Let's keep it between us, but here's something I know."

Very few people, if any, in my career have ever been able to keep confidential information to themselves. The only person I share my most confidential information with is my wife, Amy, because I know I can trust her implicitly. It's okay to share confidential information with others if appropriate, but just know there's a 95 percent chance it will get shared with someone else.

Only a Few Times in Your Life Will a Life-Changing Opportunity Come Your Way; You Have To Be Ready for It

Not too long ago, I had the opportunity to golf at Rich Harvest Farms, one of the world's most beautiful and exclusive golf courses. After our round, we attended a cocktail party where the course owner, Jerry Rich, was asked to say a few words. He was an older gentleman. It was clear he'd been very successful to have created such a remarkable golf course on his own. I love it when people like him speak because they often share pearls of wisdom.

"You may only get one opportunity in your life, be ready for it." Jerry Rich

Jerry told us about his history—how he grew up and his business journey. At the end of his talk, he gave us advice that stuck with me. He said, "At some point in a businessperson's life, there might be only one chance or one opportunity that could be the opportunity of a lifetime. Make sure you're ready for it and take advantage of it."

I reflected on this in my career and the opportunity I had to work at TriNet. It was the opportunity of a lifetime. I'm not even sure I fully understood how much of a lifetime opportunity it was at the time, but I was fortunate to have that chance and a CEO willing to take a risk on someone like me. Looking back, it was the opportunity of a lifetime and made a significant difference in my life and my family's life.

So, ensure your eyes and ears are always open, and you're ready for opportunities. You never know when one might be the opportunity of your lifetime.

Politics Versus Influence

People always tell me they hate politics. These are typically junior people with an immature view of power and influence. If you want to be an executive or a chief revenue officer, you must be a politician. However, what I call politics—and using influence—is different.

Politicians typically do things in their interest—whether to be reelected, to secure a great job after office, or to be adored by others. It's all about them; that's politics. Influence is something entirely different. Influence is using your talent, skills, relationships, and abilities to help others. This could mean advancing your organization or helping others achieve their goals. You must have influence if you want to sit at the C-level table.

People can quickly tell whether you're a typical politician or someone who uses your influence for good. The key difference is whether your actions are for yourself or others. Influence is something that should be embraced, not avoided.

What Is Your Why?

When interviewing people, I like to ask them what I call a "Columbo question." There was an old TV show called

Columbo, where the detective, named Columbo, would ask the suspect many questions. When the suspect thought all the questions were over and was ready to walk away, Columbo would say, "I have one more question." This was always the most important question, asked when the person's guard was down, thinking the interview was over.

I do something similar in an interview. I ensure there are five to ten minutes left at the end and then ask the candidate, "What is your reason for doing what you do?" Then, I pause. The candidate will have an answer eight out of ten times, but it will typically be a "what," not a "why." I follow up with, "You gave me a what, but you didn't tell me a why."

I do this because most people either won't tell you what's in their heart or aren't aware of why they truly do things. They might tell me they want to make money, advance their career, or other similar things—these are "whats"—but they don't reveal what's in their heart. Is it because they want to serve others and find great satisfaction in it? Is it because they have a sense of purpose in wanting to provide for their family so they never have to worry? Are they driven by a fear of failure or letting others down? Understanding what's in someone's heart is critical for leading them.

I ask the same question when I'm the one being interviewed. I'll ask my potential boss, "What is your reason for doing what you do?" Most interviewers and interviewees never ask this question, but I want to know what's in their hearts because that will tell me who they are.

An authentic sales leader knows their why and shares it with their team so everyone understands their motivation.

When You Want the Job, Get the Job

When I was interviewing at Google X, I decided I really wanted the job. I prepared more than I ever had for any position. On the day of my interview, I had a lunch meeting with two team members who would report to me. Both were incredibly smart and talented, though I had more experience than they did. We grabbed a beautiful sushi lunch from the Google cafeteria and brought it back to the conference room, where they proceeded to interview me.

I gave them my full, undivided attention as they asked their questions, answering each one thoroughly and respectfully. The meeting lasted an hour, and I didn't look at or touch my lunch. I wanted them to know that nothing was more important to me at that moment. After I joined the team, we laughed about how I hadn't touched my lunch. I wanted the job, and nothing would get in my way.

Bus Your Tray at Lunch

When I was at Google X, we incorporated a part of the interview process called "the meal." We would invite the candidate to have lunch with a few teammates, aiming to get them in a more casual environment to see if there was something more we could learn about them. People would invariably let their guard down while having lunch at Google, which was typically a good thing. It allowed teammates to get to know the candidate better and provide us with feedback, and it also gave the candidate a chance to get candid information about the team they were joining.

One important aspect of that lunch was the expectation at Google that you would always bus your tray when finished. It was expected that you wouldn't leave your tray or food behind and that you would clean up after yourself. We observed whether candidates cleaned up after themselves, as it demonstrated their respect for rules and attention to detail.

Unfortunately, there was one candidate we were very interested in who, after lunch, asked someone who would have been one of their peers to bus their tray for them. It was a very awkward situation, and while it might have seemed innocuous to the person asking, it ultimately signaled a lack of respect for the teammates they would join. We ultimately decided not to hire that person because of that behavior.

Take Notes in Meetings

When I'm in a meeting, I always have my notebook and pen in hand. I learned this early in my career as a sales rep. I was taught that taking notes when someone is speaking is a demonstration of respect, showing that what they're saying is important. Whenever I meet with someone, I always have my notebook ready. When I meet people who don't have a notebook, I wonder if what I'm saying is important to them. Sure, some people have photographic memories, but very few of them exist.

I love to go back to my notes because I invariably miss or forget something that was said. However, more than that, note-taking demonstrates respect. There's nothing worse than interviewing a candidate who has no notebook and isn't taking any notes during our meeting. It makes me question whether they truly care about what I'm saying and if it matters to them. Looking someone in the eye and writing something down when they speak makes them feel like you're truly listening.

Respond to One-on-One Emails

We're all busy and inundated with emails, texts, Slack messages, etc. However, when I send a one-on-one note to someone—whether asking for something, requesting feedback, or providing information—I appreciate it when they respond quickly. It can be challenging, but it says a lot about an organization when you ask for something and receive a prompt response. It suggests that this may be how they treat customers and their colleagues.

On the flip side, I make it a point to respond quickly to direct requests from my organization. It's a sign of respect. When leaders, even those several levels above, don't respond to someone, it comes across as disrespectful. No one is better than anyone in the organization. If someone is wasting my time, it's a good coaching opportunity on how to approach executives. However, it sends a powerful message when anyone can reach out to you and receive a timely response.

You Are a Corporate Athlete

One of the first things I do with teams is share an old *Harvard Business Review* article called "The Corporate Athlete." I received this article early in my career when I first became a manager. It explains that business leaders are like athletes: We're under tremendous pressure to perform; we're in the public eye and must continuously improve our results. It can be one of the most competitive jobs. There are so many similarities between an athlete and a business leader. Athletes train, take care of themselves, watch their diet, exercise, practice their craft, and work on their mental and spiritual health.

I've seen business leaders who were drunks, gluttons, cheaters, and had all kinds of vices, and eventually, it catches up with them. When their physical or mental health gets in the way of their ability to perform, it becomes a problem. I want my team to be in the best condition they can be because the better condition they're in, the better they'll be as executives. If you're tired, hungover, out of shape, or distracted, you won't be the best executive you can be.

In my book, there's no such thing as work-life balance; it's just life. Who you are and what you do in other areas of your life directly impact your business performance. So, I encourage my team to take time off to rest, exercise, and attend to their family and other important priorities. I want my people to be as healthy and happy as possible because the better they feel as corporate athletes, the better their performance will be.

11

Sales Lessons for Better Coaching

The Truth About a Deal Always Comes Out at the End

Deal reviews are meant to uncover why a deal might not happen. When you're deeply involved in a deal, it can be challenging to identify where the problems and risks lie. The best sales reps actively seek the reasons a deal might not close. The sooner you can identify these potential obstacles, the sooner you have the opportunity to address and fix them. You inevitably will find out at the end why a deal didn't happen. It's a lot like poker; eventually, everyone reveals their cards, and you discover why you won or lost.

Good Things Usually Come from Involving an Executive in a Deal

Early in my career as a salesperson, Gartner emphasized involving executives in meetings. I never fully understood why until one experience changed my perspective.

One time, I brought together two executives, one from my company and one from a semiconductor company with whom

I had been unable to progress. Despite my low expectations, my company's CEO agreed to meet with the other CEO.

On the morning of the meeting as we were doing our precall plan, my CEO said, "John, this was the one meeting I was not looking forward to." Revealing that the other executive had been his bitter rival at a previous company. As a junior sales rep, I was scared to death about what was going to happen at lunch.

However, when the meeting began, something unexpected happened. Our CEO stood up, took off his coat, rolled up his sleeves, and sat back down at the table. The other executive followed suit. This simple gesture diffused the tension, and they began discussing business.

The conversation turned out to be productive. After the meeting, I had low expectations for any immediate results. However, the following week, I received a request for a business proposal from the buyer I had been working with at the company. This led to our first closed business with that account, and they later became valuable customers.

This experience taught me the importance of involving executives in sales meetings and the power of unexpected actions to break through barriers and lead to positive outcomes.

Good things happen when you bring in an executive because executives like doing business with other executives. They understand each other's issues and know what not to ask of each other, and it typically ends up well. Later that year, at our sales kickoff, our CEO gave me a special award called the hard hat award, where he gave me a yellow hard hat for enduring such a challenging situation.

Pack Mentality

In enterprise sales, it is crucial for sales representatives to collaborate with other team members; they should never hunt alone. This includes working closely with sales engineers, executives, product managers, contract negotiators, and consultants. Teamwork is essential for effectively managing the sales process and ultimately closing deals. Lone wolves, or sales reps who work independently, often struggle to win big deals. Always sell deals as a pack.

Have a Portable Sales Process

Too many salespeople have not been taught to sell effectively. Selling is a process. Sometimes, it can be complicated. Other times, it's straightforward, but it should always be repeatable whenever possible. The best sales reps I know have a repeatable sales process they can apply to different job situations. They learn about the technology, marketplace, and issues of prospects and customers and then tailor their process to align with the buying process.

These reps know how to identify and qualify real opportunities. They understand how to question prospects to uncover their problems, envision the solutions the prospects have in mind, and create a vision match between the prospect's problems and the rep's solution. They assess whether the problem is significant enough to matter and, if so, to whom it matters and what the priority is. They determine whether it's a funded project, whether the prospect needs help securing funding, and whether they need assistance with decision-making or ensuring proper implementation.

Good salespeople know how to repeat these steps as part of their sales process. I refer to it as a portable sales process; whether it's value selling, the 5x5 process, or MEDDIC, have a process, bring it with you, and apply it. I admire reps with a track record of success and a defined way of doing things.

Do You Have a Time-Bound, Quantifiable Business Issue?

Julie Thomas, Chad Sanderson, and my ValueSelling friends taught me this. I always ask this key question at the beginning of every deal review. It's surprising how often a rep doesn't have an answer. As a business executive, I know the projects I approve and spend money on always have deadlines and specific expected business outcomes that are tied to key business priorities. This holds for all executives.

It's challenging to uncover this information when dealing with lower levels of the team because they often don't know the answers. This is one reason deals fall through: A rep may work on something someone at a lower level suggests is a priority. However, when it gets escalated to the higher-level team, it turns out not to be a key priority for the executive. As a result, it doesn't receive the funding and support needed to close the deal. This is the first question a sales rep must answer during the discovery process.

Deals Age like Fish

I've noticed that when I go to restaurants, especially steakhouses, they often talk about their aged steaks and how good they are. I guess aging helps concentrate the flavor of the meat. However, I never hear them talk about the aged fish.

Deals are similar. I've always been someone who, if a deal is on the table and close to what I want, I'll take it. I've seen too many stories where unintended situations arise—people get fired, budgets get cut, decisions change, or competitors try to undermine your deal. So, when I see a rep delaying a deal, keeping it "on the street," I encourage them to close it if it's close to our best-expected outcome. I believe that some relationship with a customer is better than no relationship.

Old Pipeline Deals are Like Dead Turtles

One of the world's greatest sales teachers told one of my favorite sales stories during an event where we had fifty people in the room. He was enthusiastic and started talking about deals stuck in the pipeline. He told an incredible story about old pipeline deals that are dead, but reps keep them in their pipelines to make them look good.

The story was about his son and his pet turtle. His son loved the turtle, but one day, it died. The father told his son the pet turtle was dead and they needed to dispose of it. His son refused and cried. The father had a great idea. He suggested they have a ceremony for the turtle, put it in a special box, bury it in their backyard, and remember it. The boy did what his father said, buried the turtle, and felt better afterward.

Old pipeline deals are the same way. A rep has put in a lot of work and created an opportunity in the pipeline; they've invested their heart and soul into it. The deal is dead, but they don't want to accept it. What I learned is that old pipeline deals are like the dead turtle. As sales managers, we should recognize the rep's hard work in the deal. We should then acknowledge that it's time to move the deal out of the pipeline and into closed lost deals.

I had one sales leader who would have a ceremony with the rep to move a deal into closed lost deals. It was kind of humorous, but it got the point across.

That Business Meal Is Not for Eating

When you go to a business lunch or dinner, you're not there to eat; you're there to work. Typically, you take someone out for a business lunch or dinner to build a relationship with the prospect. Sometimes, you'll take them to a place they would not normally go to, and they will enjoy it.

Whether I'm selling or being sold to, I know the meal has a business objective. You want to be polite and not make your guest uncomfortable. However, you want to make sure you are crystal clear on what the objectives are for the meal and what you want to get out of it.

I've seen many people in sales attend a meal like this and think they are there to enjoy a meal versus being there to sell something. I noticed this in interviews, too. When I'm interviewing for a role, and someone asks me out for a meal, I get a little disappointed because I know I won't be there to enjoy the food. I'm there to get something done. I don't like business lunches or dinners because I'd rather enjoy my meal with friends or family—without an objective.

People Buy with Their Hearts but Justify with Data

I remember sitting at a round table with ten founders of early-stage companies in the 2000s. They talked about all the great strategies for selling their products and how customers would buy them. They talked about speeds, feeds, capabilities, pricing, etc. I remember being intimidated because these people were all very smart, and I'm just a sales guy. What do I know? It finally came to me, and I said something that I don't know they fully understood, but I believe to this day: People buy with their hearts but justify it with data. Everybody talks about ROI analysis, TCO process pricing, and all these other things, but ultimately, an executive buys with their heart.

Why do I say this? When executives make purchasing decisions, they put their necks on the line. In some cases, they could be putting their job on the line. They have deeply personal reasons for what they do. It could be supporting their family, paying their bills, or keeping their self-esteem; people do what they do for many reasons. People buy things for personal reasons.

Understanding what's in a buyer's heart is a critical reason or way of understanding if you're selling something important. If it doesn't matter to them and they don't care about it, your deals are at risk. I know this is true for me. When I sit in a car I'm thinking about buying, I always imagine myself looking more handsome or smarter driving this fancy car.

Yes, I want to get a great deal. Yes, I want to negotiate something. So, I tell everybody I got a great deal, but the real reason I buy is personal. The same goes for technology sales. We all have hearts and minds.

Sales Calls: Play-by-Play and Color Commentator

Anytime more than one person is running a meeting, I like to be clear about who's doing what and what the roles are. I often ask: "Who's the play-by-play announcer, and who's the color commentator?" When you watch a sporting event, two people are typically announcing the game. The play-by-play person tells you step by step what's happening in the action, describing it to the audience. He or she sets up the color commentary to add information to the situation.

I like to run meetings the same way when I'm doing it in tandem with someone. For instance, when we're doing a sales call, I like the rep to be the play-by-play commentator or the master of ceremonies who runs the meeting. A sales manager or sales engineer is typically the color commentator, adding more depth and information to different situations during the meeting. We do the same thing when we co-lead internal meetings. I always like to know who's doing what and their roles.

A Prospect Is not a Customer

When I first became a sales leader at VERITAS, I was in a meeting, and somebody referred to a non-customer as a customer. One of the sales leaders who was quite experienced said that he didn't want anyone calling someone a customer who was not spending money with our company. They are a prospect. That stuck with me. I try to be intentional with the words I use because words matter. Therefore, I am intentional about the difference between the words prospect and customer.

It's typical for non-salespeople to call a prospect a customer, but people are not customers until they buy something from you. I want to clarify whether we are talking about a prospect or a customer. Sometimes, my teams roll their eyes, but it's an important difference to me because becoming a customer is very important to me, and I want to give my customers the ultimate respect they deserve by calling them customers.

At one company, they wanted to call prospects and future customers. I thought that was a bit cheeky and was embarrassed by that term. You're a prospect until you spend money and become a customer.

Always Be Suspicious when Things Move too Smoothly

I love selling to enterprise customers at large companies. You can make a big impact on a business and a company in this world. However, with great impact comes many risks and challenges. There are often politics within the company, competing interests, procurement people, contracts, and people who don't add anything to the process. However, they tend to shield big companies from big mistakes. You must be adept at moving horizontally within the company—not just vertically.

When a process moves too smoothly and easily, my antenna goes up. Early in my sales management career, we had a major renewal with a customer. We had multiple meetings with the decision-maker, and everything proceeded smoothly. However, something didn't feel right because they weren't utilizing the product as much as they should be. The decision maker said everything was going great, which was music to the sales rep's ears.

On the day of the renewal, we met with the decision maker to have him sign the renewal contract. We sat at his desk. We looked at him and said how excited we were to move forward. He looked at us and said, "I'm sorry to tell you this, but I've selected your competitor. We are terminating your relationship, and there's nothing you can do about it." It's a moment I'll never forget. We walked out of the meeting shell-shocked. It was a lesson to me that you should always have a healthy dose of paranoia, especially if things are moving too smoothly.

Sometimes, You Need To Back Up the Truck

When I go on a sales call, I want to know everyone's role. I want to know who will run the call; I typically refer to them as the play-by-play announcer. Then, there are the color commentators who add content, information, and expertise to the discussion. Finally, I want to know who will be coaching and watching for feedback opportunities during the meeting.

On one set of calls, I was in a team meeting with a trucking manufacturer. The sales rep was doing a fantastic job leading the call. My role as the executive was to pay attention and look for opportunities to insert an executive point of view into the conversation. However, being a salesperson at heart, I'm always looking for ways to improve the sales call. During the meeting, I noticed the prospect asked a question, but I don't think the rep caught the intent behind it. The rep started going down a different path, unrelated to what the prospect asked about. This continued for a few minutes, and I could sense the prospect's frustration growing because it seemed like the rep wasn't listening.

I don't like to interrupt sales calls unless something seriously derails the meeting. So, I decided to step in and tried to use a bit of humor by saying, "Can we back the truck up for a second?" Everyone laughed for a moment, and I revisited the prospect's question, asking, "Is this what you were asking?"

The prospect replied, "Yes, that's exactly what I'm asking." The rep took my cue, answered the question, and continued leading the meeting, which was a great success. This prospect ultimately became one of our first customers.

As a leader, sometimes it's your job to step in when things go off track during a sales call, ensuring the rep's success—even if it means backing up the truck.

Two Last Things

1. Thank you for reading this book. Reopen your book to one or two random pages, put your finger on a section, and try it.
2. Visit www.authenticsalesleadership.com for templates (the Victory Plan, How to Get an A, the Champions Guide), videos, and other free content to help you succeed as an Authentic Sales Leader.

Acknowledgments

This book is the culmination of decades spent in the trenches of go-to-market execution. From carrying a bag as a sales rep to sitting at the CEO's table as a revenue leader. My heart will always be with the Sales Reps. But I didn't do any of it alone.

First and foremost, I want to thank the many teammates, mentors, and leaders who shaped my thinking, challenged me to grow, and held me to a higher standard. Jan Rifino for originally taking the risk of hiring me into the tech industry. The sales leadership team at Gartner, led by the one and only Jay Tyler and including David Hatfield, John Besteman, Jim Blackie, Scott Mullan, Dan Heydenfeldt, and Tricia Cleary, who saw in me the talent I knew in my heart that I had. You were a one-of-a-kind leadership team.

To the leaders I had the privilege to work for. Jim Dougherty, for giving me the opportunity of a lifetime to sit at your knee and learn how a principled sales leader operates. David Hatfield for hiring me twice. Tom Kendra for saving me when I needed to be saved. John Brigden and my Symantec team in Europe, a job that started for me as a job ended up as a love affair (Neal, Derek, and the team). Burton Goldfield, for adding me to your CEO table and for believing in me despite the many mistakes I'm sure I made. Thank you for your trust, your candor, and your belief that winning is a team sport. Stephen Gillett, for your trust in me to join the team at Google X and to the Chronicle OGs; there will never be a better TEAM. Scott Brown for showing me how a leader never leaves his team behind.

To the sales operations and enablement leaders who built The Championship Program: Abbas Meghjee, Carol Sustala, Jake Goldfield, Lynn Thayer, and Matt Cox.

To the people that have influenced me throughout my career, "the padres" (Mario Prietto, SJ, Dick Cobb, SJ, Anthony Sortino, LC), the executive coaches (Mandy Flint and Isabella Conti),"the grizzlies" (Dick Boucher, Rich Moran, Rich Penrose). Kelly Kay at Heidrick, who found the gold in me. The people who help me stay healthy physically (Dr. Mike, Kim, and the Zen master) and financially (Randy Peterson). To my dear friends who encouraged me (Al B and Mo, you saw this coming long before I did).

To the founders and emerging leaders I've had the privilege of advising: your ambition and grit are contagious (Eynat, Chainsaw, Shapor, Swapnil, Grif, Randy, David). You reminded me that the playbook must always evolve and that leadership is never "one size fits all."

To the sports coaches for whom I played (Bob Drucker, Shel Zatkin Julius Yap, Aldo Congi, Leo LaRocca, Carroll Williams, Dick Davey, Pat Malley)—thank you for teaching me about resilience, discipline, and what it means to be part of something bigger than yourself. Much of what's in this book comes from lessons learned on the court and carried into the boardroom.

Acknowledgments

To my editors, reviewers, and thought partners who helped turn messy notes and battle-worn wisdom into a clear, practical guide — thank you for bringing structure to the chaos and making my words sharper, tighter, and more useful (John Rossman, Joel O'Driscoll, Chris at Jetlaunch, Eloise Cook at Pearson). Jeffrey Fox, you don't know me, but you inspired me to someday write this book.

And finally and most importantly, to my family—Amy, Zach, and Will—your love, patience, and encouragement made this book possible. You've been my true North Star, and I'm forever grateful. "La Famiglia è tutto"

This book is dedicated to the next generation of sales leaders—the ones who choose to lead with purpose, integrity, and grit. The Truth is in the Field. The world doesn't need more sales managers. It needs Authentic Sales Leaders.

Expecting great things!

About the Author

John "JT" Turner is a results-driven sales executive with over two decades of technology industry experience. He has a proven track record of leading high-performing sales teams and achieving remarkable revenue growth across diverse sectors, including cybersecurity, human capital management, and technology research.

JT's career journey is a testament to his passion for sales. Starting as a territory sales rep, he steadily climbed the ranks to become a Section 16 Officer at a publicly traded company, TriNet. Throughout his career, JT has honed his expertise in strategic planning, operational excellence, and go-to-market execution, developing a proven playbook for sales success known as the Victory Plan Playbook.

His leadership roles at prominent companies like Google, TriNet, Gartner, and Symantec have solidified his reputation as a visionary sales leader. As the global head of sales for Google Cloud Security Products, he spearheaded the expansion of the company's security offerings and built a world-class sales team. At Chronicle, an Alphabet company, JT was instrumental in developing a scalable GTM SaaS team and driving significant growth.

Beyond his sales accomplishments, JT is a dedicated mentor and coach who is committed to developing the next generation of sales leaders. He is the author of the Lighthouse management training program and has been recognized for his leadership excellence, including being named Chief Revenue Officer of the Year by *Selling Power*.

JT holds an MBA from San Jose State University and a BS in Marketing from Santa Clara University. He has also completed executive education programs at Stanford University Graduate School of Business.

A dynamic speaker and thought leader, JT is passionate about sharing his knowledge and experience to help others achieve their full potential in sales and beyond.